The Complete Book of Insurance

Understand the Coverage You REALLY Need

By Richard Wm. Zevnik
Attorney at Law

SPHINX® PUBLISHING
AN IMPRINT OF SOURCEBOOKS, INC.®
NAPERVILLE, ILLINOIS
www.SphinxLegal.com

First Edition: 2004
Second Printing: December, 2004

Published by: **Sphinx® Publishing, An Imprint of Sourcebooks, Inc.®**

Naperville Office
P.O. Box 4410
Naperville, Illinois 60567-4410
630-961-3900
Fax: 630-961-2168
www.sourcebooks.com
www.SphinxLegal.com

This publication is designed to provide accurate and authoritative information in regard to the subject matter covered. It is sold with the understanding that the publisher is not engaged in rendering legal, accounting, or other professional service. If legal advice or other expert assistance is required, the services of a competent professional person should be sought.

*From a Declaration of Principles Jointly Adopted by a Committee of the
American Bar Association and a Committee of Publishers and Associations*

This product is not a substitute for legal advice.

Disclaimer required by Texas statutes.

Library of Congress Cataloging-in-Publication Data

Zevnik, Richard Wm.
  The complete book of insurance : understand the coverage you really need / by Richard Wm. Zevnik.-- 1st ed.
    p. cm.
  ISBN 1-57248-383-0 (pbk. : alk. paper)
  1. Insurance--Handbooks, manuals, etc. I. Title.
HG8061.Z48 2004
368--dc22

                                          2004013895

Printed and bound in the United States of America.

VHG-O — 10 9 8 7 6 5 4 3 2

Contents

Controlled Substances
Contractual Liability
Owned Property
Rental Property
Workers Compensation
Nuclear
Bodily Injury to Insureds
Medical Payments Coverages Exclusions
Personal Injury Liability Coverage Exclusions
Exclusions Added by Other Insurers

Limit of Liability
Severability of Insurance
Duties after Occurrence
Medical Payments Coverage
Suits Against Us
Bankruptcy of an Insured
Other Insurance
Policy Period
Concealment or Fraud
Personal Injury Coverage Conditions
Conditions that Apply to All Coverages

Structuring Your Liability Insurance Limits

Part III: Your Auto

Structure of Personal Auto Policies
Insurable Interest
Personal Auto Policy Definitions
Liability Coverage Provisions

Family Members
Intentional Injury or Damage
Owned or Transported Property
Rented, Used, or Cared-For Property
Bodily Injury to Insured's Employees
Public or Livery Conveyances
Auto Business Exposures
Maintenance or Use of Vehicles in Business Context
Use of Vehicles without Permission
Nuclear Peril
Motorcycles and Off-Road Vehicles
Other Exclusions
Other Comments

Foreword

The purpose of this book is to demystify the world of insurance for the average homeowner, car owner and driver, and apartment renter. It is almost impossible for ordinary consumers to make genuinely informed choices without understanding how the *business* of insurance works; what the different marketing channels for selling policies are; and, what is or is not typically covered by a given kind of policy.

Unfortunately, if the wrong choices are made and a loss occurs, the consequences can be all too interesting, frightening, and life-changing. Unsuitable insurance choices present the potential of no coverage for a substantial theft or fire loss or not enough coverage for a catastrophic liability lawsuit, such as an automobile accident, that could force you into bankruptcy.

Is insurance a complete answer to all risks of adverse financial circumstances? No, of course not. But, within the realm of potential exposures to loss that the average person will face, insurance provides a relatively inexpensive way of helping to protect one's property and fortunes from ruin.

As an insurance coverage attorney, I have often seen the consequences of the failure to purchase insurance that could easily have provided protection from an avoidable, uncovered claim. Liability exposures under homeowners and auto policies present potentially great financial exposures to the average homeowner, auto owner, tenant, or small business owner.

There is the crucial requirement that you maintain adequate insurance to value. There is also a need for you to do something to document your personal property and to maintain that record in a secure place, preferably off premises, in the event of a total loss. This book will highlight many similar issues.

I mean to inform, not lecture. I am as upset and angered by claims that are mishandled as by claims in which I see denials of coverage that are correct because the policyholders were uneducated or misinformed and therefore did not purchase appropriate coverage. Too often, individuals find themselves in litigation with their insurers, their insurance agent, or both over a claim that they believed was or should have been covered. Regardless of the correctness of the insurer's claim decision, such litigation can impose financial and emotional costs on the individuals involved.

I welcome the opportunity to provide the reader with information necessary to become an informed insurance consumer, and thereby afford those readers the peace of mind that insurance is meant to provide.

DISCLAIMER

I am an attorney and work for a law firm that represents a great many insurers. Thus, the following disclaimer.

The opinions expressed throughout this book are my personal opinions, not those of the law firm for which I work, nor of any of that firm's clients: insurers, or otherwise.

I also give some examples in this book as to how certain coverage provisions may or may not apply or be interpreted. Unless the example comes from an identified court decision, these examples are purely hypothetical and should be considered illustrative only. In a real life situation, a judge or jury may disagree with how I suggest a policy provision should be understood or interpreted.

No attorney-client relationship exists, and shall not be deemed to exist, between any purchaser or reader of this book and the author, the law firm for which the author works, or of any of that firm's attorneys.

The discussions in this book are general and are intended to provide the reader with background information about various aspects of the business of insurance to assist the reader in making decisions about insurance issues. No legal advice is contained in or offered by this book, and nothing stated in this book should be relied on as such. Any reader having specific questions needs to consult with a lawyer licensed to practice in the state where the reader lives. The facts of a particular situation and the actual language of the reader's policy, interpreted according to applicable local laws, will control the outcome of any particular issue or claim.

Introduction

This book deals mainly with what is referred to in the insurance industry as *property/casualty coverages*. For consumers, this means homeowners, auto, and tenants' policies. For small business owners, this means the simpler forms of commercial policies, represented generally by so-called business owners policies. Some basic concepts of life insurance policies are explained. Disability policies, as well as health insurance policies and managed care plans, are also discussed briefly.

This book attempts to cover a huge body of information in the space of a consumer guide. Reconciling these conflicting goals was a difficult task. There are few uniform national standards or laws that apply to the business of insurance. As explained in this book, there is no single *business of insurance*. There are at least three *businesses of insurance*:

> (1) property-casualty insurance (*i.e.,* homeowners, auto, and business property and liability coverages);
>
> (2) life and disability insurance; and,
>
> (3) health insurance.

The first category is the primary focus of this book. This category of coverages is largely regulated by the fifty states. The second category, life insurance, is also largely regulated by the fifty states, except to the extent the investment aspects of certain types of life insurance policies implicate federal securities laws.

The third category of insurance discussed in this book, health insurance, is now largely regulated by the federal government. States can, and in some instances, do, impose regulatory requirements over and above those of federal law. This book will largely limit itself to the discussion of significant health insurance issues arising under the controlling federal laws.

This book is mostly about the coverages of the policies that matter most to the average personal insurance buyer: personal auto policies; homeowners, condo owners, and tenants policies; and, business owners policies.

As discussed elsewhere, the business of insurance is far-reaching and affects almost every business or personal economic transaction that takes place in the world. Even though insurance is an important subject, most law schools in the United States do not have any significant, realistic, or practical courses in the law of insurance. If you read this book in its entirety, you will learn more about insurance than the average new law school graduate knows.

This book is about empowerment. It is about giving the consumer the ability to penetrate the often opaque business of insurance, particularly homeowners and personal auto insurance, and to provide the reader with the information with which to make intelligent decisions when it comes to choosing an agent and purchasing coverage.

Let me first tell you, the reader, what this book discusses, and how it relates to the insurance-buying decisions you face. This book discusses and explains the principal coverages of the *Insurance Services Office's* (ISO) homeowners and personal auto policies.

So what, you say. I have my homeowners and auto insurance with State Farm, Allstate, Liberty Mutual, Nationwide, or Farmers. The importance is, ISO is an insurance industry support, rating, and information organization. The policy forms developed and published by ISO are used by many insurers without alteration. Other insurers, like several of those just mentioned, use policy language drafted by ISO, or language that differs in varying, but usually small, degrees from the language of the ISO policies. However, it would expand the scope of this book to enormous proportions to detail all of the differences between standard ISO policy forms and those of the major personal lines insurers mentioned above.

Even though insurers, particularly personal lines (*i.e.*, homeowners and auto coverages) insurers, want to create the appearance that their products differ from one another, as a practical matter, they want their policy language to compare (on a general basis, at least) with that of the ISO forms so as to take advantage of court decisions interpreting the ISO policy provisions. Doing so at least permits predictability when it comes to adjusting claims.

This book discusses the coverages of the ISO homeowners and personal auto policies so that the reader/consumer has a basis for questioning his or her agent regarding the coverages of the insurer or insurers the agent represents and how they may differ from those of the standard ISO forms. As noted, many insurers use the ISO policy forms. Several national personal lines insurers, however, do not. Although the coverages afforded by policies issued by insurers that do not use ISO forms usually depend largely on language similar to the ISO forms, the differences in the scope of coverage afforded can vary widely from insurer to insurer. Mere differences in price are not a valid basis for comparison between the policies of one insurer and those of another. The differences in the scope of coverage can be astounding in their details—details that can be significant to the consumer.

This book is intended to provide the reader with something he or she has not had before—the basis for genuine comparison shopping for something that we all must buy, but is all too often poorly understood. It comes down to this simple proposition—if homeowners and auto insurance policies are things you must buy, don't you want to get the most coverage for the least money? The existing system does not provide the consumer with the ability to engage in informed comparison shopping. This book is intended to rectify that situation.

Finally, while this book does not address all the issues that can arise in the claims context, there is some discussion about claims issues integrated into corresponding discussions of policies.

PART I: Insurance and You

Chapter 1

The Role of Insurance in the Economy

Insurance. What a pain! Your mortgage lender requires that you carry fire and other perils coverage (*i.e.*, homeowners) insurance and sometimes even flood or earthquake insurance. Your auto lender requires that you carry physical damage coverage. Under the laws of many states, you are required to carry auto liability and/or *no-fault* liability insurance, often including *uninsured* motorist and *underinsured* motorist coverages.

To many, insurance just represents dollars out of pocket with no benefit. This is an unfortunate attitude. Insurance plays a broad role in the worldwide economy, helping to assure that millions of transactions and other activities, economic and noneconomic, can proceed.

Without insurance, local, state, national, and international business would quickly grind to a halt. Lenders would cease lending for purchases of land, buildings, homes, vehicles, or equipment. Without premises liability insurance, a simple slip-and-fall claim could put a small business owner out of business.

Manufacturers could not sell products without liability insurance to respond in the event a defective product injures customers or other users of their products. Absent product liability insurance, a seller of a defective product who has no role in the design and manufacture of the product, could face a ruinous lawsuit or judgment.

The average individual has similar concerns. What are the consequences of an uninsured liability lawsuit—whether rising from an auto accident or a premises claim arising from homeownership question? The answer is often bankruptcy, which can follow a person for a lifetime. It can result in being turned down for a job, being denied credit, or receiving credit only at high interest rates.

The concept of insurance is really very simple. In exchange for the insured's payment of a relatively small sum of money—the *premium*—the insurer assumes the risk of financial consequences for the loss of the insured's property (such as a house or car) or the risk of the loss presented by the costs of defending a liability lawsuit (and where appropriate, paying a resulting settlement or judgment). This can provide financial security for the average consumer—that is *you*—which strengthens our economy as a whole and spurs further growth.

BRIEF HISTORY OF THE BUSINESS OF INSURANCE

Insurance has been around for a long time and has been a part of the economy of the world and this nation since before it *was* this nation. Frankly, the United States, as an indirect product of the initial commercial-empire building activities of Great Britain, owes its existence to the business of insurance in large part. Great Britain became a major commercial power in the 17th century, based on the risks taken by companies established to capitalize on the demand for spices, tea, sugar, dyes, fabrics, and other desired commodities.

The business of insurance as we know it in Great Britain and the United States grew out of what initially was risk-taking participation in the fruits of those commercial enterprises. It evolved to insure the risks of loss of or damage to cargoes.

The insuring entity, known commonly as *Lloyd's of London*, grew up out of those risky commercial endeavors. Lloyd's of London is an exceedingly complex organism. Lloyd's is not a company, nor is it an insurer, nor a broker. Lloyd's is an insurance market where persons known as underwriters, or underwriting syndicates, participate in providing insurance for risks pre-

sented to them by Lloyd's brokers. The Lloyd's brokers in turn have corre-
spondent relations with insurance brokers worldwide. The aspects of
commerce out of which Lloyd's grew continue to be a basis for the business
of insurance, and the insurance markets in London, including Lloyd's, remain
major players in the world's insurance markets.

A second major aspect of the development of the business of insurance
found its roots in the growing peril of fire as urban centers developed in
Great Britain and later in the American colonies. No running water existed
at the time; construction was essentially unregulated. Even a small fire posed
the risk of spreading rapidly.

The burden of response to fires and the risks posed by fires in such envi-
ronments was addressed in a variety of ways. One was the mutual fire
protection societies in given areas of large cities. Members maintained fire
buckets in their houses and businesses and pledged to assist in fighting fires
when they occurred. This included the physical participation in fire fighting—that is, working as part of *bucket brigades* when fires broke out.

From these societies, two principal offshoots emerged as the world entered
the Industrial Age. These were:

1. the growth of volunteer, and later, professional, paid fire
   departments and
2. the increased growth of these fire insurance societies and later,
   commercial insurance companies that grew out these societies.

The fire insurance societies evolved from merely providing mutual aid and
assistance in the event of fire to providing limited financial protection in the
event of a fire loss. However, due to the localized nature of these fire insurance societies, they could not obtain the spread of risk necessary to the
financial viability of the concept of insurance. Since all the properties insured
were in relatively close geographic proximity to each other, the risk of a single catastrophic fire that could overwhelm the physical ability to combat the
fire existed, as well as the financial resources to fulfill the indemnification
payment for loss of all members.

Nonetheless, with a number of developments—satisfactory water supplies; improved municipal regulation of construction (such as early set-back laws); regulation of permissible roofing materials; and, more careful risk selection, including the avoidance of insuring too many closely situated properties—the fire insurance business began to grow and flourish. As with so many other aspects of commerce, with the opportunity for profit, new insurers were established to compete for property owners' business.

As the business of insurance in the United States grew, it also diversified. Due to the importance of agriculture to the United States economy—and the fact that in the 19th and first half of the 20th centuries, agriculture was conducted largely by means of family farms—lenders required farmers to take out crop insurance when mortgaging their properties to obtain crop loans. This requirement greatly expanded the use of insurance.

Then, as you might expect, some of the biggest boosts to the growth of the business of insurance came with the development of the internal combustion engine, the widespread ownership of cars and trucks, and the risks of loss that operation of these vehicles posed.

There are, of course, other contributing threads. As society and industry grew, so did the risk of industrial injury and the resulting passage of workers compensation laws. When those laws were enacted, commercial insurers entered the market and began providing workers compensation insurance to employers.

The growth of our rail system also spurred growth of the insurance industry. The railroads provided transportation, but their operation created risks of losses due to fires from sparks thrown out of smokestacks of locomotives, and from collisions and derailments.

The business of insurance has continued to evolve. Recent times have seen the development and marketing of long-term care insurance, environmental impairment insurance, and insurance policies aimed at e-business. In e-business, exposures to loss often involve less risk of damage or destruction of tangible property in the commonly understood sense, but rather risks of economic losses as the result of deprivation of service due to the activities of hackers, for example.

As human economic activity evolves, so will the business of insurance. Likewise, while coverage questions arise under existing policies based on the facts of novel claims and courts render decisions, policy language will continue to evolve.

Coverage for some kinds of losses will always be clear—it will clearly exist or not exist. Claims in the gray areas will be decided one way or the other and will shape that which the average insurance buyer should or should not reasonably expect to be covered under his or her policies.

Chapter 2

The Structure of the
Business of Insurance

The business of insurance differs from most other businesses. Because insurers sell an intangible product—a promise to pay in the event of contingent losses—and because these promises potentially affect so many, the business of insurance is regulated more heavily than most other businesses.

The business of insurance is regulated by the states, not by the federal government (with the exception of certain antitrust laws). As a result, while there is necessarily much uniformity of regulation in the business of insurance from state to state, there are also differences.

NOTE: *For any state-specific question, contact the department of insurance in your own state.*

The laws regulating the business of insurance in some states differ so greatly from other states that many insurers establish separate companies solely for the purposes of writing policies in a given state. Texas and Illinois are two states where this often occurs because of the difficulties imposed by complying with the laws of those particular states.

Twelve states mandate some form of no-fault auto insurance. As a result of these differences, certain types of policies, particularly auto policies, must be written so that people can travel from state to state in their vehicles, yet not run the risk of uninsured losses due to variations in mandatory insurance requirements by state.

Because of state regulations and other business concerns, a given insurance organization typically comprises multiple insurers. State Farm advertises nationally on television and through other media, but the organization operating under the State Farm moniker is actually comprised of twelve different insurance companies, each separately organized. Indeed, many of the separate insurance companies operating under a single trademark or service mark, such as State Farm, Farmers, Kemper, or Nationwide, have officers and a board of directors, but no actual employees.

There are a number of practical reasons why many insurance organizations do business in this manner, which vary from organization to organization. Some states' insurance codes and regulations are such that a given insurance organization will establish an insurance company solely for the purposes of writing all of its policies for insurance within a particular state. Another reason an insurance organization might establish multiple insurance companies to operate within a given state is to help the insurance organization track and assess business results.

These business factors (and more), even before looking at the actual loss experience of an individual insured, can affect whether an insurer will categorize the insured as a *preferred* risk, a *standard* risk, or a *substandard* risk. Depending on how an insurance organization decides it wants to compartmentalize its ability to track its results, it may choose to do so based on a *preferred*, *standard*, or *substandard* risk basis, regardless of the line of business. It may establish separate companies in which to write policies issued to each of these categories of its business.

KINDS OF INSURERS

The most common form of organization for domestic insurers is the capital stock company (*corporation*) organized and existing pursuant to the laws of whichever of the fifty states is its corporate domicile. The stock of individual capital stock insurance companies is not always publicly traded. Often, insurers are wholly-owned subsidiaries of one or more other insurance companies comprising a given insurance organization. For example, the group of companies known as American International Group, Inc. (AIG) owns, directly or through subsidiary companies, such well-known commercial insurers as National Union Fire Insurance Company, American Home Assurance Company, Lexington Insurance Company, Insurance Company of the State of Pennsylvania, and Birmingham Fire Insurance Company. The parent company of this group is the corporation known as American International Group, Inc. This corporation is not an insurer itself. Rather, it is what is commonly referred to as a *holding company*. If a person wished to invest in the insurance business of the AIG companies, one would buy stock in American International Group, Inc. One could not purchase stock directly in any of the member companies that comprise AIG.

The corporate domicile of a particular insurer may or may not be the same state where that particular insurer has its principal place of business. Just because an insurer is organized and exists as a legal entity under the laws of a particular state, and may even have its principal place of business in that state, does not mean that the insurer operates as an *admitted insurer* in that state. Insurers can be organized and exist pursuant to the laws of a particular state, and yet operate within that state on a nonadmitted (excess or surplus lines) basis.

The next most common form of insurance company organization is the *mutual* insurance company. Stated generally, a mutual insurer is an insurer corporation without capital stock that is owned by its policyholders collectively, who have the right to vote in the election of its board of directors. The principles governing the duties, powers, and obligations of the board of directors of a mutual insurer are generally the same as those applicable to other private corporations.

Many insurers that retain the word *mutual* in their names have long-since converted to the capital stock form of doing business. They retain the term *mutual* in their corporate names not only because of the company's history, but also because the use of the term *mutual* has a feel-good quality that helps support the image of security that insurers like to promote.

The third most common form of insurance company organization is what is called a *reciprocal insurer*, also called *interinsurance exchange*. In effect, all policyholders of a reciprocal insurer, who are also called *subscribers*, insure each other. In order to become an insured of a reciprocal insurer, each person or company executes a *subscription agreement* as part of the application for the policy. In the subscription agreement, that person or entity appoints an attorney-in-fact, who, pursuant to the terms of the subscription agreement, manages the affairs of the reciprocal insurer. The attorney-in-fact is often a separately constituted corporation. Through the corporation's employees or through contractual relationships with other entities, the attorney-in-fact arranges for underwriting, actuarial, claims, and other services, and enters into reinsurance contracts.

For example, the insurance offered by the American Automobile Association or its affiliated organizations in different states, such as the Automobile Club of Southern California, is offered through entities that are organized as reciprocal insurers. United Services Automobile Association is another well-known example. Reciprocal insurers are often organized and will insure only those persons who share some qualifying membership criteria, such as a club membership or service in the armed forces.

All three types of insurance companies are regulated in substantially similar fashion by the insurance departments of the fifty states. Mutual and reciprocal insurers give their policyholders the right to appear and vote at the annual meetings of insurers, just as stockholders of a corporation have the right to attend annual meetings and to vote to elect directors and pass resolutions on the agenda. This is a right that relatively few policyholders take advantage of.

Both mutual and reciprocal forms of insurance company organizations are, in a certain sense, vestiges of a past world in which a relatively small group of localized individuals came together to create a means of providing insurance to an unserved or underserved group of people or businesses. The voting rights aspect of these insurance company organizational forms reflects the different practicalities confronting those persons that, as a small group of affected policyholders, the acts of the board of directors of the company affects directly.

As a practical matter, the differences between capital stock, mutual, and reciprocal insurance organizations affect the average consumer very little, except in the manner in which insurance is sold.

The following comments are somewhat more true of reciprocal insurers than they are of mutual insurers, but nonetheless may apply. The policies offered by reciprocal and mutual insurers are often less expensive than those offered by stock insurers. That factor has been one of the perceived historical advantages that reciprocal and mutual insurers hold over stock insurers. In the past, their cost advantages had much to do with the fact that the underwriters and actuaries for such insurers had a good understanding of the risks posed by the limited classes of individuals to which policies would be issued and the limited geographical scope of the insurers' operations.

However, the less expensive nature of the policy sold by reciprocal and mutual insurers can be very deceptive in the modern-day world. Reciprocal and mutual insurers developed at a time when the world was much simpler. When everyone was selling nothing more than a standard fire policy, with the terms and conditions of the policy mandated by state law, all insurers were, in effect, selling the same *promises*. At that time there was a basis for a localized reciprocal or mutual insurer to offer savings to policyholders that mattered.

As society and insurance markets matured, that was no longer the case. Today, homeowners policies offer coverages that go beyond those of standard fire policies. The insurance purchaser needs to compare coverages offered and included (or not included) to determine whether the lower premiums often offered on policies of reciprocal and mutual insurers can be justified by the sometimes lesser coverages offered compared with those of other companies, including stock companies.

Chapter 3

The Marketing and Selling of Insurance

All too often consumers are led into purchasing policies that do not provide even remotely sufficient insurance to protect them from the effects of reasonably anticipated losses. It is crucial that you understand insurance well enough to be able to ask the necessary questions so you can assess the abilities of the potential insurance agents you contact and can help whichever agent you ultimately choose to procure insurance appropriate to your needs.

There are three primary marketing channels of property and casualty insurance, particularly homeowners and personal auto insurance, in the United States. They are:

1. independent agents;
2. captive agents; and,
3. various forms of direct marketing.

This latter category includes what nominally appears to be a variety of marketing channels often using direct mail. These channels are employed by GEICO, Progressive Casualty, certain American International Group mass-marketed insurances, often by direct mail, as well as other regional and national carriers, such as 21st Century Insurance (a primarily personal auto insurance carrier operating in California, Arizona, Nevada, Washington, and Oregon).

In some cases, a given insurer may employ multiple marketing channels.

INDEPENDENT AGENTS

An *independent insurance agent* is a person who is licensed by the department of insurance in the state (or states) where he or she conducts business. Licensure generally involves passing a written examination to show that the person meets minimum standards of knowledge regarding the business of insurance.

Independent agents are typically parties to contracts with several insurers by which the agent is authorized to write business (*i.e.,* policies) for that insurer. In most states, each insurer files a notice of appointment of each agent with the department of insurance in that particular state. Independent agents are usually compensated by the insurers they represent through payment of a commission that is a fixed percentage of the premium of each policy sold. This commission percentage may vary with the size of the premium or line of business. For example, insurers often pay higher commissions on commercial lines policies than they do on personal lines policies. This is due in part because the underwriting and production of personal lines policies is often less complex, presenting fewer variables, and typically involves smaller premiums per policy. The administrative costs to the insurer of issuing a commercial policy for a small business and a personal lines policy are roughly the same.

Independent agents frequently state that one advantage of dealing with an independent agent is that he or she often has the flexibility to obtain competing quotes from several insurers. These competing quotes may offer the insured broader or lesser coverage in response to greater or lower premiums, thus offering the insured a range of choices.

An independent agent will not have a State Farm, Farmers, Allstate, or Nationwide logo in their Yellow Pages ad, or over his or her office. Independent agents are often members of professional/trade organizations, such as the *Professional Insurance Agents* (PIA) organization or *Independent Insurance Agents* (IIA) organization. Their advertising in the Yellow Pages and otherwise will usually make clear that they are independent agents, especially the fact that they represent several companies. In some regions, the Yellow Pages will have listings of agents who represent particular insurers that conduct their business even though they are independent agents—so checking by a particular name, such as *Hartford* or *Kemper*, may help you identify local independent agents.

CAPTIVE AGENTS

Captive agents represent only a single insurer. In some instances, they may even be employees of the insurer. Examples of captive agents are agents who sell State Farm, Allstate, Nationwide, and Farmers policies. A State Farm agent, for example, is limited to offering the policies offered by the State Farm companies. If a given customer seeks a type of insurance not offered by a captive agent insurer, the customer will end up having to go to another agent or broker to obtain a quote or a policy.

Nonetheless, the captive agent manner of marketing of insurance, particularly personal lines policies, obviously has been successful. State Farm, Allstate, Nationwide, Liberty Mutual, and Farmers control a substantial portion of the United States personal lines insurance market.

However, if you really want to comparison shop for competing quotes involving considerations other than price from several companies, including from one or more captive agent companies, you will have to contact an agent from each company separately and compare the results on your own.

The most important thing the consumer needs to do is locate a competent agent. While there is no single yardstick by which to gauge an agent's competence, things to inquire about include:

- ◆ education level (*i.e.,* is the agent in question a college graduate?— sometimes the ability to spot issues is crucial);
- ◆ how many years of experience does the person have as a licensed agent?;
- ◆ whether the agent is a member of any of the professional insurance associations. While not a perfect measure, such memberships can indicate a level of knowledge and commitment to a business and career; and,
- ◆ whether the agent has a chartered property casualty underwriter (CPCU) designation.

NOTE: A CPCU designation is earned by completion of a series of college-level courses in various aspects of the business of insurance and by passing a nationally administered examination for each of the required courses. CPCU designations are sought and earned by many insurance industry personnel, such as underwriters and claims representatives, in addition to agents and brokers. Holding a CPCU designation is considered within the business of insurance a mark of commitment to an insurance career and a significant professional achievement within the business.

There are competent and professional agents who are independent agents, and who are captive agents. You just need to understand enough about the various marketing channels to make a decision which form makes the best sense for you.

DIRECT WRITERS

As our economy and markets have changed, other insurance marketing channels have developed. While these alternate marketing channels for insurance initially focused on motor vehicle insurance, more recently they have expanded to include homeowners insurance as well.

The problem with these direct marketers is that there is no practical ability for the average insurance buyer to compare the terms and conditions of the policies offered in order to determine whether or not the coverages offered meet the needs of the insurance buyer. And there is no one to provide any counseling with respect to decisions involved in the purchase. You do not have the ability to call on the services of an agent to help you choose the policy limits appropriate to guarantee that you have sufficient coverage to repair or replace your residence and possessions in the event of a major loss.

Many of the 800-number or Internet sellers of insurance have engaged in widespread television advertising of their policies. These TV commercials frequently emphasize potential premium savings as the inducement to buy that company's policies. *Premium savings* does not mean much without advice about variations in optional coverages or how much in limits the average person needs to purchase for adequate protection.

These direct sales operations present a potential trap for the unwary by creating a serious risk of uninsured or underinsured loss exposures. A particular disadvantage of many such direct marketing insurers is that there is often little or no opportunity to review the policy forms utilized to determine whether they contain unanticipated restrictive terms. Certainly, in order to be licensed to sell policies in any particular state, the policies' terms necessarily will be in compliance with that state's minimum requirements. However, that does not ensure that such policies will necessarily provide the best coverage for your particular needs.

Compounding this problem is that most insurers charge a penalty if a policy is issued and then cancelled at the insured's request midterm.

EXAMPLE: You purchased a one-year policy and cancelled it after two weeks because you discovered it contained restrictive terms that did not provide coverage for a particular loss exposure. In this situation, you will receive a refund that is less than fifty-weeks worth of the premium. Unless a direct marketing insurer offers the opportunity to examine the policy in advance or offers a no-charge return policy, you might want to pass. Instead, avail yourself of the services of a local agent you can meet in person and discuss your insurance needs with to obtain the best compromise between cost and extent of coverage provided.

RETAIL VERSUS WHOLESALE BROKERS

Many insurance consumers will never need to deal with the concept of *retail brokers* versus wholesale brokers. An insurance broker is the agent of the insured and can submit applications for coverage to insurers for which the broker does not have an agency appointment.

Some insurers will only accept applications from a broker with which they have an agency relationship. In addition, coverages can be placed with non-admitted insurers only through an excess or surplus lines broker.

A *wholesale broker* is a broker involved in the procurement of a policy that does not have a direct relationship with the insured. For example, an applicant for a personal auto policy might not be an acceptable risk to standard carriers due to a variety of underwriting factors, such as age or poor loss history (*i.e.*, excessive number of citations or accidents). The problem is, in many states, surplus lines regulations and statutes are not scrupulously observed. And, when they are not, it is usually to the average consumer's disadvantage. If an insurance agent you may have turned to suggests that he or she is going to provide you with a quote or recommends that you purchase a policy through a nonadmitted insurer (a surplus lines broker), you should start asking some pointed questions as to why.

A policy issued by a nonadmitted insurer in your jurisdiction is not protected by your state's insurance guaranty fund. In the event that insurer becomes insolvent, your policy is *worthless*. For the sake of some premium savings, you are completely unprotected in the event of insolvency of a nonadmitted insurer.

When you place insurance with an admitted insurer, you are protected up to the limits established by your state's insurance guaranty fund in the event your insurer becomes insolvent. In general, that means you get a lawyer appointed to defend you if you get sued and a covered judgment or settlement will be paid up to the covered statutory limits of your state's guaranty fund. It also means that your covered automobile physical damage claim or claim for damage to your house or possessions will be paid, subject to the statutory limits.

For example, in California, under Insurance Code section 1063, the maximum amount of a claim payable by the California Insurance Guaranty Fund is $500,000. That is an amount sufficient to cover most serious liability claims that the average homeowner is likely to face. It also is an amount sufficient to cover many partial losses to a residence and contents, even though, in the face of escalating construction costs, it may not, in some cases, be sufficient to cover total losses.

There is a reason why one of an insurance agent's most essential functions is to place coverages on behalf of their customers with insurers that are financially strong. This is because the amounts typically available in the event of insurer insolvency under the various states' insurance guaranty funds may be less than the loss exposures of many insureds.

State laws exist that require warnings to the insurance purchaser of the risks involved in purchasing insurance from a nonadmitted carrier. However, few, if any, brokers involved in the sale of such policies generally warn of or explain these risks and the trade-offs involved to their customers adequately. This is particularly true in the personal auto liability coverage context, where these abuses are most prominent.

A far too common circumstance, particularly in major urban areas, with large numbers of *substandard risk* insureds, is for high-volume brokers to run mass-marketed commercials, promising to be able to provide auto insurance to *anyone*, and at great savings. Such mass marketers of insurance often emphasize that coverage can be available for low down payments, and low monthly payments. These representations are often highly deceptive. Such operations often sell ridiculously expensive, low-limits policies, often issued by nonadmitted insurers. Rarely do such operations inform their customers of their state's *assigned risk* programs, which, if applicable, usually provide better coverage than that from a nonadmitted insurer.

Unfortunately, the fact is that while certain high-risk insureds may need to consider purchasing insurance from nonadmitted insurers, these insureds are usually commercial insureds with higher exposure to risk and loss histories—individually or as an industry classification. This leaves them perceived as high-risk from an underwriting standpoint. The average personal auto or homeowners insured should rarely be in such a position.

Other disadvantages exist using a nonadmitted insurer. Nonadmitted insurers prey on persons who have been advised that they are substandard risks, particularly in the personal auto context. The claims service offered by nonadmitted insurers is generally poor or nonexistent. They offer and sell policies that are often apparently cheap (compared with the premiums that would be charged by an admitted insurer) and they let the insured nominally satisfy their state's financial responsibility/proof of insurance laws. However, their promises are often functionally smoke and mirrors.

An insurer that does not pay claims promptly or does not step in and defend an unsured when he or she has been sued has given none of the protections expected by someone who has purchased an insurance policy. It does you little good when you are faced with a lawsuit resulting from an accident to find yourself having to fight a two-front war—one against the person suing you and a second against your insurer to obtain the coverage that you paid for.

Brokers that routinely place personal lines policies with nonadmitted carriers may argue that they are saving their customers money. These claims are usually illusory. In most cases, however, the premium savings do not offset the risks of an uncovered loss in the event of insolvency of the insurer, or in the case of a nonadmitted insurer simply failing to observe its policy obligations. Many nonadmitted insurers are domiciled outside the United States, making suing them and recovering an uncertain proposition.

There is almost never any need for an individual or a family to turn to a surplus lines/nonadmitted insurer for personal auto or homeowners insurance. Many states have what are called *alternative market* mechanisms.

Examples of such *alternative market* mechanisms are automobile *assigned risk* plans, and *FAIR* plans. (FAIR refers to fair access to insurance requirements, under the plan established under the California Insurance Code.)

Under such plans, all admitted insurers writing automobile or property insurance are required to participate or fund these plans. In the case of most *assigned risk* auto insurance plans, when a person qualifies (usually by virtue of proof of refusal to issue a policy by a certain minimum number of insurers), he or she is assigned to an insurer that must issue a policy. This is subject to such policy limit and premium limitations as may be established by the plan.

Nonetheless, the ability to purchase a policy through an assigned risk plan guarantees that an individual is going to be able to obtain coverage from a standard lines admitted carrier. Assigned risk plan policies are more expensive, but the insured has the security of coverage with an admitted insurer. If the policyholder *cleans up* his or her loss, violation, or infraction history, he or she can eventually purchase coverage in the standard insurance markets and will no longer need to rely on coverage through an assigned risk plan.

FAIR plans are alternative market mechanisms for hard-to-place home-owners or other property insurance polices. These are used in areas such as Southern California, urban areas that are underserved by standard lines insurance markets, and other areas that are considered higher than normal risk (such as homes located in and near *brush* areas). Again, the issuers of policies offered through these types of programs are entitled to charge premiums that reflect the increased risk assumed. However, for most persons, policies procured through such plans are preferable to policies from nonadmitted insurers. This is due to the protections afforded by the fact that these policies are covered by each state's insurance guaranty funds and because of better and more reliable claims service.

GUARANTY FUNDS

Each state has an insurance *guaranty fund*. Each operates in substantially the same way. In the event of insolvency of an insurer whose policies are covered by the guaranty fund (*i.e.,* an admitted insurer in that state), policyholders of that insolvent insurer are covered up to the statutory limit. This limit varies from state to state, but is sufficient to cover most anticipated property claims and all the genuinely catastrophic liability claims. In addition, the guaranty fund statutes provide for defense of liability claims in addition to paying judgments or settlements up to the amount of the statutory limit.

The protection offered by the guaranty fund is not perfect protection. But, the protection offered is far better than having none and is a substantial reason to purchase insurance coverage from an admitted insurer as opposed to a nonadmitted insurer.

Guaranty funds are funded by you and every other policyholder in your state. You are all providing protection for each other. The initial capitalization (*i.e.,* start-up funds) for guaranty funds comes from assessments of all admitted insurers doing business in that state, in proportion to the respective amount of premiums written by each insurer in that state. Under the guaranty funds statutes of all states, the insurers that have paid these assessments to provide the start-up capital to establish the guaranty fund were, and are, entitled to recover the costs of those assessments. This is recovered by premium surcharges on all of their policyholders. If you were to examine your premium billing notice over a period of time, you will notice such surcharges, typically between $1 and $5. This charge is imposed by your insurer proportionately on all of its policyholders to cover the costs of assessments it has been obligated to pay to fund the guaranty fund in your state.

The guaranty fund in each state operates much like an insurance company. Guaranty funds set reserves, retain defense counsel, and settle and defend claims. They also adjust property claims. The primary difference is in the source of their funding. Insurance companies fund their operations primarily by charging premiums and by realizing investment income on their reserves (premium reserves and loss, loss adjustment expense, and other reserves). Guaranty funds likewise generate income by investments received on reserves. They do not have, however, premium income as a source of income. Nor do guaranty funds have the overhead associated with marketing and selling policies, as do insurance companies.

When an insurance guaranty fund needs to generate income because the claims it has paid are depleting it imposes assessments on all admitted insurers doing business within the state.

CHOOSING WHAT IS BEST FOR YOU

A good independent agent is likely to be the best place for most insurance consumers to start. By employing an independent agent, you preserve the maximum number of options for yourself. And, you are less likely to find yourself in a situation in which you have insufficient limits or unexpected gaps in insurance coverage in the event of a major loss.

This is particularly true if you are the owner of a small business. The underwriting of commercial insurance policies is inherently more complex than is the underwriting of personal lines policies. Independent agents are much more likely than captive agents to have a substantial volume of commercial business in addition to their personal lines book of business. Consequently, a good independent agent is likely to be much more attuned to the inquiries necessary to assure that your coverages are as complete as possible and to avoid coverage gaps. This is particularly true with respect to the form of and the amount of business interruption insurance, plus additional, optional commercial coverages, that may be appropriate for you.

These are some common examples of situations where a good independent agent's skills are important. For example, a developer might want its own coverage to apply only as excess coverage over its coverage as an additional insured under the policies of the subcontractors working for it on a construction project. The knowledge of the developer's loss exposures and the ability to assure that those loss exposures are covered appropriately requires expertise that is often beyond that of an agent for a direct writer.

Similarly, a vendor might want the coverage of its own policy to apply only as excess coverage over its coverage as an additional insured under a manufacturer's policy for product liability suits brought against the vendor by a purchaser of an alleged defective product made by that manufacturer. Again, effecting the insurance needs of such a vendor requires a certain level of knowledge and expertise that may be beyond that of many personal lines oriented agents.

The choice is yours. The important point is for you to realize that you have a choice and that exercising that choice means that you need to better inform yourself so that you obtain the protection best suited to your needs.

Chapter 4
Insuring Other Interests

Everyone understands that the fundamental concept of buying insurance is to protect one's own financial interests. What is not well understood is that our legal relationships with others create obligations to protect their financial interests as well. When we assure that those legal obligations are taken care of, we secure our own financial well-being.

Once this abstract discussion is reduced to everyday terms, the concept does not seem so strange. These are relationships of great importance to individuals and businesses in their everyday lives and activities and one's insurance decisions are interwoven with these relationships. These relationships can include:

- ◆ mortgage lenders on your home;
- ◆ lenders on your auto loan;
- ◆ lenders on other items, whether as lenders or lessors on contracts for business equipment; and,
- ◆ persons with whom you have contracted to sell goods or to provide goods and services, who require that they be named as additional persons insured under your policies.

MORTGAGES OR TRUST DEED HOLDERS

If you live in the eastern states, you recognize the former concept—*mortgage.* If you live in the western states, where there is a different legal usage, you recognize that the lender on your home is a *holder of your trust deed* as the security interest on your home loan. Either way, the fundamental concept is the same. You, the named insured under your homeowners policy, have a home loan. You want to insure your interest in your home. Your home loan lender, which holds a security interest in your home to the extent of the unpaid loan balance, wants you to assure that you insure your home so as to protect its security interest. Not only that, your lender *requires* that you do so and that you cause it to be named an additional insured in the loan documents of your home loan.

It is very important for you to make sure that your homeowners insurer:

- ◆ is always timely and promptly informed of who your home loan lender is, what their appropriate address is, and what your loan number is;
- ◆ shows your home loan lender on your policy as an additional insured to the extent of its interest in your property; and,
- ◆ supplies your home loan lender with evidence that they are an insured *every year* at the time your homeowners policy is renewed.

Most homeowners insurers are pretty good about assuring that your home loan lender receives evidence of insurance on renewal each year. That does not, however, mean that you do not need to make sure that they do. It is possible for your insurer to become confused as to who your current mortgage lenders are that need to be shown as additional insured interests on your policy, particularly when many individuals are refinancing their home loans at frequent intervals or are taking out second mortgages or home equity lines of credit. There can be potential adverse consequences to you if your home loan lender does not receive evidence of insurance each year at your policy's renewal. These potential adverse consequences to you make your attention to assuring that this detail is attended to each year necessary.

If your lender does not receive timely evidence that its security interest is not insured, your loan documents permit your lender to place insurance—*solely to protect its interests at your expense*—through its own master insurance program. It can also charge the costs—not just the premiums, but also the administrative costs—to your loan.

This is something you do not want to happen. First, you are only digging yourself in deeper with respect to the amount of your outstanding loan balance.

Second, the insurer with which your home loan lender places such *forced coverage* is often an affiliate or a subsidiary of the lender. Do you think that the premiums charged by such an insurer are going to be competitive with the premiums you could obtain in the marketplace with respect to your own policy? Think again. They have an inherent profit motive and conflict of interest, but one that your contract with your lender—and the law— supports. They have no reason to charge a competitive premium for such force-placed coverage.

Third, the terms of coverage are limited and favor only the lender. You get something only if they have managed to insure for a sum greater than the amount of the outstanding loan balance—something that rarely happens. Your home loan lender does not have an insurable interest in your property in an amount greater than the amount of its outstanding loan balance.

Fourth, these *forced placement* policies do not cover your personal property (*i.e.,* your contents). In the event of a loss, you are on your own.

Fifth, defaulting on your obligation to insure your property and failure to have your home loan lender named an additional insured on your homeowners policy to the extent of its interest can be reported as a breach of your obligation under your home loan. This can result in a negative (and serious) credit report that can affect your ability to obtain other credit.

If you are a homeowner, and have a first, second, or third home loan, mortgage, home equity line of credit, or any other credit facility that is secured by your house, condominium, or farm, you need to make certain that your lenders' security interests are protected by appropriate endorsements to your policy. You need to make sure that your insurer knows of the existence of all of these interests, the address of each of the lenders in question, the loan number, and the need to make sure that all secured parties receive annual evidence:

- of the fact that you continue to maintain property insurance on the property in which they have an interest;
- that the amount of the insurance you maintain is sufficient to protect its interests (*i.e.,* the total amount of outstanding loans); and,
- that each such secured party is an insured under your policy.

AUTO LESSORS AND LENDERS

Regardless of where in the United States you live, if you are leasing a car or a truck or are making payments on a vehicle purchase loan, the leasing company or auto loan finance company will include as a contract provision the requirement that they be shown as an insured party on your automobile policy. Your auto lease or loan contract may even specify the minimum coverages you are obligated to maintain (typically collision and comprehensive coverages).

The lease or auto loan contracts often give the lessor or lender the right to place coverage to protect their interest in the event of loss (but not your interest) and to charge you for the cost of such coverage. This will happen unless you make sure that your auto insurer provides evidence of coverage at each policy renewal.

Usually, notifying your insurer is done at the time the lease or loan documents are signed. Many automobile dealers will not release a vehicle to a customer until the dealers have confirmation that your insurer has been informed of your lease or purchase of a new vehicle. It is often a dealership's finance department that undertakes this notification, based on information supplied by the customer.

However, it is usually a better practice for you to call your insurance agent and personally provide him or her with the new vehicle purchase or lease information. It is better to take the responsibility to handle the notification yourself and to make sure it is done right.

Even if you do not have all the information needed (such as the correct legal name of the lender or its address), you can at least tell your agent the name of the dealership, its telephone number, and the name of the correct person at the dealership to contact in order to obtain the financing and additional insured information necessary. This will guarantee that the auto leasing company or automobile finance company is properly included as an insured party under your automobile policy.

If you are trading in a vehicle as part of the transaction or if you have sold it in a private party transaction, you will need to call your agent to advise him or her of that change to the policy. Also, if you pay off any outstanding loan balance, then you will need to notify your agent that the prior lender should be deleted from your policy.

When in doubt, more notice to your agent (*i.e.,* both from you and from the auto lender) can never hurt. It is only a failure to give notice or complete and accurate information to your agent that can lead to trouble.

OTHER SECURED PARTIES

As individuals, your mortgage (including home equity lender) and auto lenders are the most common entities you will need to assure are added as insureds under your insurance policies. If, however, you run a business and have policies for your business, you may encounter circumstances in which you need to add other persons or companies to coverage as insureds under your policies.

ADDITIONAL INSURED INTERESTS UNDER LIABILITY COVERAGES

The preceding sections deal with additional insured interests under policies covering items of real and personal property. There are circumstances, usually limited to commercial policies, in which a policyholder may need to add another person or business as an additional insured under the policies' liability coverages. Common situations in which this can occur include a wide variety of circumstances.

◆ Construction contractors may be obligated under contracts with property owners for whom the contractors are performing services to add the owner as an additional insured under the contractors' policy for liability arising out of the contractor's work for the owner. Similarly, construction subcontractors may be contractually obligated to add the developer or general contractor they are performing services for as an additional insured for liability arising out of the subcontractor's work.

◆ Persons who lease business premises may be obligated to add the owner of the premises as an additional insured for liability arising out of the use and occupancy of the premises pursuant to the lease.

◆ Churches and charitable organizations may obtain additional insured endorsements extending coverage to officers, trustees, board or vestry members, or volunteers in other roles, while they are acting in their respective capacities for the church's or organization's activities.

There is a wide variety of standard form additional insured endorsements, including, in some cases, more than one form that may apply to a particular situation. If an inappropriate version of such an additional insured endorsement is obtained, the person or company to whom you owe the obligation to procure additional insured status may not receive the expected coverage. It could result in that person or company turning to you personally for the costs of the defense in the event of lawsuit or for paying a claim in the event of a loss that would have been covered if the correct form of additional insured endorsement had been employed.

It is beyond the scope of this book to detail all the different types of additional insured endorsements available or to detail when a particular form of additional insured endorsement is more appropriate than another in a given circumstance. In order to help ensure that you obtain the correct additional insured coverage for your particular circumstances, it is important that you provide as much information as possible to your agent or broker. This may include copies of your leases or contracts with parties who require additional insured status under your policy. This will help to assure that the correct or most appropriate additional insured endorsement is added to your policy and that the person or other company added as an additional insured is correctly specified. It is also important to specify the activities for which additional insured status is sought so the additional insured is not receiving coverage that is broader than that required by the terms of the lease or contract in question.

Finally, for some persons or entities that are receiving coverage as additional insureds under the policies of another person or company, it is necessary that they inform their own agent or broker of that fact, so that he or she can take appropriate steps to coordinate the coverages. Specifically, if a person or company is an additional insured under the policy of another, the insured may want that additional insurance to apply to claims or lawsuits as primary insurance. In those situations, it would want the coverage of its own policy to apply only as excess coverage, that is, only after exhaustion of its coverage as an additional insured under the other party's policy.

PART II: Your Home

Chapter 5

Homeowners Insurance

What most people think of as homeowners insurance really is composed of several categories that include policies intended for:

- owners of single-family residences, including duplexes and triplexes where the property owner occupies one or more dwelling unit (*i.e.*, homeowners policies);
- owners of homes that are not single-family residences, but rather where there are multiple units in a given building, where the building is jointly owned by the owners of individual living units (*i.e.*, condominiums, townhouses, and cooperatives); and,
- tenants policies.

Each of these categories of policies is structured and organized in the same overall fashion. That basic structure follows, with detailed information regarding specific parts discussed later in detail. First, the policy's *declarations* appear, where the subject matter of the coverages afforded are stated. This material includes:

- the name of the insurer;
- the policy number;
- the inception and expiration dates of the policy (*i.e.*, the policy period);

- the named insured;
- the named insured's mailing address, and if different, the address of the premises insured;
- the policy limits applicable to:
  - the property coverages;
  - the liability coverage; and,
  - the medical payments coverage;
- the deductibles;
- the forms and endorsements comprising the policy; and,
- in states requiring that the agent countersign the policy, the agent's countersignature.

In addition, most states require that the declarations of the policy issued by nonadmitted insurers (that is, excess or surplus lines insurers) must inform the insured that he or she will not be protected by that state's insurance guaranty fund in the event of insolvency of the insurer.

The policy's *definitions* section often follows, although some insurers' policies reserve the definitions for the last section of the policy. Personal lines policies more commonly place the definitions at or near the beginning of the policy, with commercial lines policies placing the definitions at or near the end of the policy.

The policy's property coverage provisions appear next, which are usually presented in the following order. The *insuring agreements* (or coverage grants) appear first. There are typically separate insuring agreements applicable to:

- the dwelling and separate structures;
- personal property; and,
- additional living expense.

The *exclusions* applicable to each of these subsets of coverages appear next. In most cases the need for a separate listing of exclusions applicable to the building and contents coverages is pretty obvious. Exclusions fall into two primary categories: perils (*i.e.,* risks of loss) not covered and types or items of property that are not covered.

The policy's *conditions* specifically applicable to the property coverages appear next. Policy conditions generally state acts that must be done or that the insured must refrain from doing in the event of a claim in order for coverage to exist. Policy conditions can also set forth items such as the manner in which claims will be valued, dispute resolution mechanisms, or may provide procedural mechanisms for how losses will be paid in the event of death or incapacity of the insured. There is usually a separate list of conditions that apply only to the liability coverages and another list of policy conditions that apply to both the property and the liability coverages. The most important typical conditions are highlighted later.

The policy's *liability* and *medical payments coverage* provisions appear next, and are usually presented in the same order as just outlined for the property coverages. First, the liability and medical payments insuring agreements (also known as coverage grants) are stated. The statement of these insuring agreements often includes the description of so-called *additional coverages*. In some circumstances, the statements of these additional coverages follows, rather than precedes, the exclusions.

The *exclusions* applicable to the liability and medical payments coverages are stated. These exclusions are often broken down into several categories or groups, such as:

  ◆ the exclusions applicable only to the liability coverages;
  ◆ the exclusions applicable to both the liability and the medical payments coverages; and,
  ◆ the exclusions applicable only to the medical payments coverages.

The *conditions* applicable to the policy's liability and medical payments coverages are next stated. One of the most important groups of conditions applicable to the liability coverages is the one stating the insured's duties in the event a third party sues or makes a claim against the insured. It is key if someone makes a claim against you or sues you to notify your insurer immediately. Keep copies of all demand letters you receive and all legal papers that are served on you. Give copies of these documents to your insurer promptly when it asks for them. Do not discuss the claim or the lawsuit with the person who is making the claim or suing you, nor with that person's attorney. Do not admit liability. Do not make any payments to the person who is suing you without the advance knowledge and consent of your insurance company. Such payments might later be characterized as an admission of liability. Your insurer should hire a lawyer to defend you. If you hire your own lawyer before the insurer hires a lawyer to defend you, the fees charged by your lawyer may not be covered.

Most policies' basic coverage forms conclude with a section that contains the *conditions* that apply to both the property and to the liability coverages.

Finally, your policy probably will contain a number of *endorsements* that add to, delete, or modify provisions contained in the basic policy form. Endorsements are usually one, two, or three pages long each. Insurers use endorsements in order to reduce the administrative costs of reprinting their entire policy form in order to incorporate these new or changed provisions. Often, endorsements are used to restate a policy provision after a court decision interprets the provision in question in a manner different from how the insurer believed it should have been interpreted.

Commonly, endorsements add exclusions not stated in the basic policy form. These often include exclusions for such things as sexual molestation, physical abuse, or mental abuse of minors; home daycare services performed for a profit; and dog bites.

The following chapters discuss the principal coverages of the standard HO 2 and HO 3 homeowners policy forms published by the *Insurance Services Office* (ISO). ISO is an insurance industry support organization that develops rates and policies. Most insurers' policies rely heavily on ISO policy language, even if they do not actually use ISO policy forms.

PROPERTY COVERAGES UNDER HOMEOWNERS POLICIES

First-party property coverages provide for indemnification to the insured, for damage to or destruction of *covered property* by an insured peril. There are several concepts set forth in the previous sentence. First, there is the concept of *insured capacity.* In order to be entitled to payment under the first-party property coverages of a homeowners, condominium owners, townhouse owners, or tenants' policy, the person seeking payment must qualify as an insured.

Second, there is the concept of *insurable interest.* In order to be entitled to payment under the property coverages of a homeowners policy, the person seeking payment must not only qualify as an insured but also have an ownership or other insurable interest in the damaged or destroyed item of property. Although people commonly speak of property insurance as insuring property, it actually does not. Rather, property insurance policies are personal contracts between the insured and the insurer. The insurer is actually insuring the insured's pecuniary interest in property. This pecuniary interest in property of an insured person is the concept of insurable interest.

Third, the item of damaged or destroyed property for which a loss payment is sought under the property coverages of a homeowners policy must qualify as *covered property* (see p. 43).

Fourth, in order for payment to be made for damage to or destruction of an item of *covered property*, the loss to the property must be the result of *covered peril. Perils* are active physical forces, fortuitous (that is, unexpected or unintended) in nature, that damage or destroy property.

INSURED CAPACITY: NAMED INSUREDS

Commonly, more than one person qualifies as an insured under a policy. The person named in a policy's declarations is the *named insured.* The named insured under the policy has greater rights and responsibilities than other persons who may also qualify as insureds.

Insured Capacity: Other Persons Insured

The policy's definitions sections will define who, other than the named insured, may qualify as persons insured under a homeowners policy.

For example, your mortgage lender is added to coverage as an additional insured to the extent of its security interest in your house, condominium, or townhouse. This is generally the outstanding loan balance. A mortgage lender is usually added to coverage under an insurance industry standard endorsement or provision known as a *standard mortgage clause*. Sometimes the language of the standard mortgage clause is included directly within the policy form, as opposed to being added as an endorsement to the policy.

The definition of *insured* under the ISO standard HO 3 homeowners policy includes such persons as:

- the named insured and his or her relatives who are residents of the named insured's household;
- nonrelatives of the named insured under the age of 21 who are residents of the household and are in the care of the named insured; and,
- full-time students who were (a) residents of the named insured's household before moving out to attend school, and (b) relatives of the named insured, and (c) under the age of 24, or (d) in the care of a named insured or a relative resident of a named insured and under the age of 21.

The persons insured provisions of homeowners policies issued by insurers that use their own forms may differ. Depending on your particular circumstances, the definition of who does and does not qualify as an *insured* under different insurers' policies may be of importance to you. For example, some insurers' homeowners coverage persons insured definitions do not extend insured capacity to students off premises. Thus, if you have a child away at school or college, his or her personal property may not be covered if your policy does not include your child as an insured person while away at school or college.

What is most important to note is that residents of a household who are not relatives of the named insured and who are (a) over 21 and (b) not in the care of a named insured do *not* qualify as insureds. An example of this would be if the named insured is renting a room to a boarder or is letting a nonrelative live on the insured premises without charge. In this situation, that person's property (*i.e.,* his or her clothing and other possessions) is *not* covered by the named insured's homeowners policy, because such persons do not qualify as persons insured.

Insurable Interest

In order to qualify for coverage under the first-party property coverages of the homeowners policy, a person cannot simply qualify as an insured. He or she also must also have an *insurable interest* in the damaged or destroyed property for which payment of a loss is sought.

This principle is perhaps best illustrated by considering the situation of a mortgage lender that is an insured under a homeowners policy issued to the borrower on the home loan. The mortgage lender has a security interest in the residence to the extent of the outstanding balance owed by the borrower. By virtue of the mortgage clause in the homeowners policy, the mortgage lender has an insurable interest in the residence and is entitled under the policy to be named as a payee on any check issued by the insurer for damage to or destruction of the home. The mortgage lender does not, however, have an insurable interest in the home as to any sums payable for damage to or destruction of the residence that exceed the outstanding loan balance. Nor does the mortgage lender have any insurable interest in the homeowner/borrower's personal property and is not entitled to payment for damage to or destruction of the borrower's personal possessions.

Covered Property

Answering what is *covered property* is generally easy. It will be set forth in your policy. As to the *dwelling* and *other structures* (some policies use the term *separate structures*) portion of the ISO HO 3 policy, the policy does not cover *land*—including the land on which the dwelling or other structures are located. Under the *other structures* coverage, other structures that are rented or held for rental to any person who is not a tenant of the dwelling are not covered. There is an exception to this provision for other structures rented for use solely as a private garage.

Nor does the other structures coverage apply to structures from which any *business* is conducted. The clear import of this limitation, which corresponds with several other policy provisions discussed later, is that homeowners policies are intended to cover risks of loss incidental to the personal use and occupancy of a dwelling and associated other structures—not an insured's *business* activities. If an insured has business-related loss exposures, the insured needs to buy a separate business or commercial policy to cover those nonpersonal, business loss exposures.

What constitutes *covered property* under the personal property provisions of a standard ISO HO 3 homeowners policy is defined by three separate categories. These are:

1. covered property;
2. property which is covered, but for which the policy establishes strict limits on the dollar amount of coverage; and,
3. property that is not covered.

The concept of covered property is stated broadly initially and is then limited by the two sections of the policy that follow. In other words, the boundaries of coverage are defined more by exclusions than they are by the grant of coverage itself.

Covered property is personal property owned or used by an insured anywhere in the world. In addition, after a loss (and at the insured's request), coverage extends to personal property owned by others (including a guest or *residence employee*) while that personal property is located on the *residence premises* occupied by an insured.

There are limits on claims made for property not located on the residence premises. Exceptions are made to these limits for personal property that is moved from the residence premises because the residence premises is being repaired, renovated, or rebuilt and for personal property in a newly acquired personal residence. The exception for a newly acquired personal residence is only good for thirty days from the time the insured begins to move the personal property from the current residence to the new residence.

Low Limit Covered Property

There are several categories of *covered property* that are made subject to rather low limits. Most homeowners insurers will insure these categories of property for higher limits at a higher premium. These categories of personal property for which coverage is afforded subject to sublimits are:

- a $200 sublimit on cash, bank notes, bullion, gold, silver, platinum, coins, metal, scrip, stored value cards (*i.e.,* electronic gift cards), and smart cards;

- a $1,500 sublimit on securities, accounts, deeds, evidences of debt (*i.e.,* promissory notes), letters of credit, manuscripts, personal records, passports, tickets, and stamps, regardless of the medium (paper or computer software) on which this type of material exists;

- a $1,500 sublimit on watercraft, including their trailers, furnishings, equipment and outboard engines or motors;

- a $1,500 sublimit on trailers or semitrailers used for items other than watercraft;

- a $1,500 sublimit for loss by theft of jewelry, watches, furs, or precious or semi-precious stones;

- a $2,500 sublimit for a loss by theft of firearms and related equipment;

- a $2,500 sublimit for loss by theft of silverware, silver plate, gold ware, gold plate, platinum ware, platinum plate, and pewter, including flatware, hollowware, tea sets, trays, and trophies;

- a $2,500 sublimit on property located on *residence premises* that are used primarily for *business* purposes;

- a $500 sublimit on *business* property away from *residence premises* except as described in the following two categories;

◆ a $1,500 sublimit on electronic apparatus and accessories while in or on a motor vehicle, but only if the apparatus is equipped to be operated by power from the motor vehicle's electrical system even though capable of being operated by other power sources; and,

◆ a $1,500 sublimit on similar items as described in the preceding paragraph while away from *residence premises* but while not in or on a motor vehicle, with the same operating power limiting language.

This is an area in which comparison of the coverages offered by insurers using the ISO HO 3 homeowners policy, as opposed to proprietary policy forms, may make a difference to you. There is a great deal of variation from insurer to insurer, both in the magnitude of the sublimits their policies provide and the categories of property that are subject to such sublimits.

The policies offered by some insurers provide broader coverage than that of the ISO HO 3 policy. Other companies' policies provide lesser or narrower coverage. This is one of the areas in which comparison shopping and research may be of value to you. The more coverage you can get without the need to schedule certain categories of property, potentially the better for you. On the other hand, scheduling property that may be difficult to value in the event of loss provides the protection of an agreed amount of coverage in the event of loss. The ultimate decision depends on the extent and value of your personal property possessions that may fall into the categories of property subject to these sublimits.

No Coverage

Under the standard ISO HO 3 homeowners policy, certain categories of personal property receive no coverage. These are:

◆ articles separately described and specifically insured, regardless of the limit for which they are insured under any other insurance (to avoid double recovery);

◆ animals, birds, or fish;

- motor vehicles and accessories, equipment, or parts while they are in or on the motor vehicle;
- aircraft (not including model or hobby aircraft not intended to carry people or cargo);
- hovercraft, flare-craft, and air-cushion vehicles;
- property of roomers, boarders, or other tenants, excepting property of roomers or boarders who are related to an insured;
- property located in an apartment regularly rented or held for rental to others by an insured;
- property rented to or held for rental to others off the *residence premises*;
- business data, regardless of whether stored as paper, electronic, or computer records;
- credit cards and electronic fund transfer cards, except as otherwise covered. (See the discussion of *Additional Property Coverages*, p.59.)

Perils Covered

Although it is something of a misnomer, the *real* property coverages of all the homeowners policies discussed (as opposed to *personal* property coverages) is so-called *all-risk* coverage. Under all-risk policies, coverage is defined by the policy's *exclusions*. The typical all-risk property insuring agreement provides that the insurer insures against *risk of direct physical loss to property....* This means the risk of loss to dwellings and separate structures.

Most homeowners insurers also sell *named perils* policies, in which covered property is only covered if loss results from a specifically listed peril. Such named perils policies are usually less expensive than the all-risk policies sold by the same insurer. This is true both of insurers that use standard ISO policy forms, as well as insurers that use proprietary policy forms.

As noted at the beginning of this section, the term *all-risk* policy really is a misnomer. This is because the all-risk coverage of such policies only applies to dwellings and separate structures. The property coverage applicable to personal property is *named perils* coverage in most cases.

There are really two functional differences between all-risk coverage and named perils coverage. First, as noted, under all-risk coverage, direct physical loss to covered property is covered unless the cause of loss is excluded. Under named perils coverage, covered property is only covered if loss is caused by a peril that is specifically listed in the policy. The real difference here is that, in a practical sense, the list of covered perils under an all-risk policy is more inclusive than under a named perils policy.

Second, whether a policy is an all-risk or named perils policy affects the burden of proof in the event there is a coverage dispute after a loss that results in a lawsuit between the insured and the insurer. Under the laws of most states, the insured of an all-risk policy need show no more than that damage to or destruction of covered property occurred. The burden of proof then shifts to the insurer to prove that an exclusion precludes coverage.

In the world of property insurance, the terms *peril*, *risk*, and *risk of loss* refer to fortuitous, active, physical forces, such as fire, lightning, windstorm, theft, and vandalism (just to give a few examples). The concept of risk or peril as an active physical force is pretty self-apparent. The condition of fortuity requires a bit more explaining: *fortuitous* means *occurring by chance* or *accidentally.* For example, damage to property caused by wear and tear or failure to maintain is not loss that occurs by chance. Loss due to normal wear and tear is deterioration through use—a certainty, not a fortuity.

The fortuity requirement precludes coverage for intentional damage or destruction of property. This is why, for example, arson is not covered. There is another reason why intentional damage to or destruction of property is not covered. If such damage was covered, it would create an undesirable incentive for insureds to destroy property for the purposes of generating cash when they found themselves in financial difficulty.

Covered Locations

Before discussing covered and noncovered perils, an explanation is needed regarding the geographic reach of coverage. As noted, the personal property coverage of most homeowners policies is worldwide. Most homeowners policies also afford coverage to locations other than simply the residence premises in the policy's declarations.

This can be seen by reviewing the policy's definition of *residence premises* and *insured location*. In the standard ISO HO 3 (and the HO 2 named perils policy as well), *residence premises* means:

- ◆ the single family dwelling that the named insured resides in; *or*,
- ◆ a 2-, 3-, or 4-family dwelling in which the named insured resides in one or more of the dwelling units; *or*,
- ◆ that part of any other building where the named insured resides; *and,*
- ◆ which is shown as the residence premises in the policy's declarations.

This definition is clear that residence premises is just *one* place—the place specified in the policy's declarations. The definition of *insured location*, however, makes sure that coverage extends to other locations as well. *Insured location* includes:

- ◆ the residence premises;
- ◆ other premises, other structures, and grounds used by the named insured as a residence and which is either:
  - ▪ shown in the policy's declarations or
  - ▪ which the named insured acquires during the policy period for use as a residence (in practical terms if, for example, you have a second or vacation home, that second or vacation home would be covered if it were listed in your policy's declarations);
- ◆ any premises used by the named insured in connection with either of the two preceeding categories of *insured location* (*e.g.*, a storage facility);
- ◆ any part of the premises that are not owned by the named insured at which the named insured is temporarily residing;

- vacant land, other than farmland, that a named insured owns or is renting;

- land that is owned by or rented to the named insured on which the named insured is building a one, two, three, or four unit residence for him- or herself or for another insured;

- individual or family cemetery plots or burial vaults of an insured; and,

- any part of premises occasionally rented to an insured for other than *business* use (*e.g.*, if you were to rent a vacation cabin or cottage for a few weeks, it would qualify as an insured location).

Named Perils Policies

Most all-risk homeowners policies are just *sort of* all-risk, because their coverage for contents/personal property is named perils coverage. There are exceptions, however. The personal property/contents coverage of some carriers' policies is all-risk coverage. This is an example of how an insurer may seek to compete with other insurers, including direct writers, by offering broader coverages at a comparable price.

It is differences like this that make comparison-shopping between homeowners policies of various companies difficult unless you have taken the time and trouble to have educated yourself. For example, if a direct writer's policy's contents coverage is named perils coverage, that insurer's agent, who only represents a single insurance company, would be unlikely to point out the differences between the coverage of the policies offered by the company he or she represents and one offered by a company whose homeowners policies include all-risk coverage on contents. Unless *you* know the difference and can assess that difference in terms of a potential noncovered loss exposure, you cannot make an informed decision.

Whether you have a named perils or all-risk homeowners policy, you are protecting your dwelling, other structures, and personal property from the following covered named perils.

- *Fire and lightning.*
- *Windstorm or hail.* There are some important limitations to this covered peril. Coverage exists for the interior of buildings or the contents within a building caused by rain, snow, sleet, sand, or dust, unless the direct force of wind or hail first damages the building, causing an opening in the roof or wall through which entry of the rain, snow, sleet, sand, or dust enters. This restriction has tended to preclude coverage for rain, snow, sleet, sand, or dust damage that is the result of poor maintenance or that is caused by leaving doors or windows open.
- *Explosion.*
- *Riot or civil commotion.*
- *Aircraft (including self propelled missiles and spacecraft).* This is actually a more common cause of loss than you might imagine. Think of how many news reports you have seen in your lifetime about a private airplane that has crashed and damaged or destroyed one or more homes.
- *Vehicles.* There is an exception to this peril. No coverage exists to fences, driveways, or walkways caused by a vehicle that is owned or operated by a resident of the residence premises. Note that this exception applies only to these three limited categories of property. If you or another resident of your household has an accident and causes vehicle damage to your dwelling or garage, that damage will be covered.
- *Smoke.* Here again, there is some qualifying and limiting language. *Smoke* means the sudden and accidental damage from smoke, including the emission or puff back of smoke, soot, fumes, or vapors from a boiler, furnace, or related equipment, but does not include loss caused by smoke from agricultural smudging or industrial operations. If you experience a fire loss, or if a neighbor experiences a fire loss and you suffer resulting smoke damage to your house or contents, that smoke damage will be covered.

◆ *Vandalism and malicious mischief.* These two terms are essentially duplicative. Under the law of most states, if a word or phrase used in an insurance policy is not specifically defined, its meaning is determined by reference to dictionaries of ordinary usage. Therefore, if you see a word or a phrase in a policy and the policy does not define that word, check the dictionary. The vandalism and malicious mischief coverage does not apply if the dwelling has been vacant for more than sixty consecutive days immediately before the date of loss. This vacant property limitation does not apply to dwellings that are in the course of construction.

◆ *Theft.* The theft coverage is subject to several qualifications. First, the peril of theft includes attempted theft. This recognizes that an unsuccessful attempt to steal an item of property nonetheless can result in damage to or destruction of property. For example, you scare off a burglar who is trying to steal your television and the burglar drops the television, destroying it. Theft also includes loss of property from a known place when it is likely that the property has been stolen. In other words, no one witnessed the disappearance of an item of property, but theft is the most likely explanation. For example, you discover that your lawnmower is missing from your unlocked garden/tool shed where you normally keep it between uses. However, the peril of theft does not include loss caused by theft:

  ■ committed by an insured;

  ■ in or to a dwelling under construction or of materials or supplies used in construction until after the construction is complete and the dwelling is occupied; or,

  ■ from that part of residence premises that is rented by an insured to a person who does not qualify as an insured. (This is yet another provision that reinforces the notion that a tenant's personal property is not something that the named insured under a homeowners policy has an additional interest in. It also reinforces that if you have a tenant, the tenant must procure his or her own insurance for his or her personal possessions in order to protect them from the risk of loss.)

◆ *Falling Objects*. You might think for a moment, *that sounds like a rather odd peril. What might a loss caused by a falling object entail?* They are actually more common than you might expect. For example, if you live below a hillside with rocky soil, under the influence of heavy rains, a large rock might dislodge from the hillside and roll downhill, striking your residence. The damage resulting from that descent is clearly fortuitous and would be covered.

◆ *Weight of Ice, Snow, or Sleet.* This peril does not include damage to buildings or contents other than from the weight of ice, snow, or sleet itself. For example, damage to the dwelling or contents caused by a roof failure due to the weight of accumulated snow would be covered. Resulting water damage to the interior or contents caused by the melting of snow subsequent to the roof failure may not be covered. Nor does this peril apply to loss to awnings, fences, patios, pavements, swimming pools, foundations, retaining walls, bulkheads, piers, wharves, or docks.

◆ *Accidental Discharge or Overflow of Water or Steam.* This is a pretty complicated covered peril. The manner in which this peril is stated in the current ISO HO 2 and HO 3 policy forms has been substantially clarified as compared with previous versions, particularly with respect to a topic that has received a lot of publicity in recent years—the subject of coverage for claims of mold damage and mold contamination.

This peril is defined as *accidental discharge of water or steam from within a plumbing, heating, air conditioning, or fire protective sprinkler system or from within a household appliance.* This peril expressly provides that the terms *plumbing system* or *household appliances* does not include a sump pump or related equipment or a roof drain, gutter, downspout, or similar fixtures or equipment. What is not made clear is what a plumbing system does or does not comprise. Whether a plumbing system includes both pressurized supply lines and fixtures, and nonpressurized drain and toilet lines is ambiguous.

This peril also includes as covered the cost to tear out and replace any part of the dwelling or other structure when it is necessary to do so in order to repair the system or appliance from which the water or steam has escaped. This tear-out-and-replacement coverage only applies to other structures if the water or steam causes actual damage to a building on the residence premises.

The accidental water or steam discharge coverage does not apply if the dwelling has been vacant for more than sixty consecutive days prior to the loss. Company specific proprietary policies may vary in terms of the length of this time period.

Nor does the accidental water or steam discharge peril include the cost of repair of the system or appliance from which the water or steam escaped. This peril also does not cover loss caused by or resulting from freezing, except as is provided for in the separate enumerated peril of *freezing.* Nor does it cover loss on the residence premises that is caused by an accidental discharge or overflow that occurs off the residence premises.

Finally, the current ISO HO 2 and HO 3 policy forms state that the accidental water or steam discharge peril does not include loss *caused by mold, fungus or wet rot unless hidden within the walls or ceilings or beneath the floors or above the ceilings of a structure.* The intent of this provision is to limit coverage for loss caused by mold to circumstances in which the mold growth or damage is not reasonably apparent to the insured. If an accidental water discharge occurs, the elimination of coverage for loss caused by mold or fungus provides an incentive for the insured to take prompt action to remove the escaped water and to repair water damage so as to prevent the growth of mold in the first place. Mold can only grow in an environment where there is a constant source of water—for example, where there is a repeated or continuous leak or seepage from a plumbing line or drain, such as beneath a kitchen sink.

In effect, the manner in which this provision is now drafted strikes a reasonable balance for an insured's expectations of coverage between a covered accidental water discharge loss and an uncovered loss that is the result of long-term neglect or failure to maintain the premises on the part of the insured. Many of the mold growth and contamination cases that have received attention in the news media have arisen from neglect or failure to maintain situations, rather than from accidental discharge of water or steam situations.

◆ *Sudden and Accidental Tearing Apart, Cracking, Burning, or Bulging.* This peril affords coverage for direct physical loss caused by the sudden and accidental tearing apart, cracking, burning, or bulging of a steam or hot water heating system, air conditioning system, an automatic fire protective sprinkler system, or an appliance for heating water. Again, this peril contains an exception for loss caused by freezing, except as provided for in the separate peril of *freezing*.

◆ *Freezing.* This peril affords coverage for loss caused by freezing of plumbing, air conditioning, fire protective sprinkler systems, or household appliances only if the insured has used reasonable care to maintain heat in the buildings or shut off the water supply to all such systems and appliances. Again, this peril provides that plumbing systems do not include sump pumps, rift drains, gutters, or downspouts.

◆ *Sudden and Accidental Damage from Artificially Generated Electrical Current.* This peril is defined more in terms of what it does not include than what it does include. It states that it does not include loss to tubes, transistors, electronic components, or circuitry that are a part of appliances, fixtures, computers, home entertainment units, or other types of electrical apparatus. In short, this peril covers direct physical loss to the dwelling or contents (other than electronic devices) that results from power surges or arcs, such as, for example, fire, explosion, or smoke damage.

◆ *Volcanic Eruption.* This peril is fairly self-explanatory. It does contain an express limitation excluding loss from earthquakes, land shock waves, or tremors. Earthquake is a commonly excluded peril from standard property policies, both personal lines and commercial lines policies. In areas that are subject to earthquake, earthquake insurance can be purchased, usually in the form of an endorsement to a policy or as a separate earthquake damage policy. In addition, from a practical standpoint, geographic areas that are at risk of a volcanic eruption loss are seismically active, and therefore also are reasonably susceptible to earthquake losses. It can be imagined that in the right confluence of circumstances, a volcanic eruption loss might present some loss adjustment challenges if the volcanic eruption was accompanied by sufficiently strong earthquakes that may have caused or contributed to the damage.

Chapter 6

Loss of Use
and
Additional Coverages

Before discussing the exclusions (Chapter 7) applicable to the property coverages of homeowners policies, there are two additional categories of property coverage grants that need to be discussed. These are:

- loss of use coverage and
- miscellaneous additional coverages, frequently grouped under a heading in the policy referring to *additional coverages* or *additional protection.*

LOSS OF USE COVERAGES

The loss of use coverages fall into three general categories:

- additional living expense;
- fair rental value; and,
- loss due to civil authority.

In general, in order for loss of use coverages to be triggered, there must first be a covered loss to residence premises. In other words, a covered loss of use must be a consequence of a covered direct physical loss to residence premises.

Additional Living Expense Coverage

Under the ISO HO 2 and HO 3 homeowners policies, if a loss covered under the policy's dwelling coverage renders the part of the residence premises where the insured resides unfit to live in, the insurer will pay *any reasonable increase in living expenses incurred by the insured so that the insured's household can maintain its normal standard of living.* The insurer will make the additional living expense payments for the shortest time required to repair or replace the damage or, if the insured permanently relocates, the shortest time required for the insured's household to settle elsewhere. These time periods are not limited by the expiration of the policy.

In some states, these time periods are made subject to an objective standard. In other words, the shortest time to repair or replace the damage would be the time that an objectively reasonable contractor would require to complete the repair or replacement work. In other states, the time period during which additional living expense payments will be made is held to be governed by what circumstances are or are not within the insured's control. Such circumstances could range from the unavailability of materials or the unavailability of a qualified contractor, to a dispute with the insurer over coverage for the damage to the residence, which delays the repair work.

Fair Rental Value Coverage

Fair rental value coverage applies when there is covered damage to that part of residence premises that the insured rents or holds for rental to others that render the premises unfit to live in. The insurer will pay the fair rental value of the premises, less any expenses that do not continue while the premises remain unfit to live in. Such fair rental value payments will be made for the shortest time required to repair or replace the premises.

The same issues exist as to whether the shortest time required to repair or replace the damaged premises is governed by a theoretical objective standard or by some other standard that takes into account other factors.

Civil Authority Loss of Use Coverage

Under this coverage, additional living expense or fair rental value coverage is available for no more than two weeks if civil authority prohibits the insured from use of residence premises as a direct result of damage to neighboring premises by an insured peril. The loss of use coverages further provide that no coverage exists for loss or expense due to cancellation of a lease or other agreement.

The loss of use coverages of homeowners policies issued by insurers that do not use the standard ISO HO 2 or HO 3 policy forms often are substantially similar to the standard form policies. Some insurers impose a 12-month maximum period for which additional living expense or fair rental value payments will be made. Others do not include such a fixed maximum period of recovery limitation.

Some insurers' policies base the availability of loss of use benefits due to order of civil authority on the existence of direct damage to a neighboring property that would constitute a *covered loss* under their respective policies. Others do not use the covered loss to adjoining property limitation at all.

ADDITIONAL COVERAGES

Homeowners policies contain several *additional coverages*, some of which relate to and are dependent on the existence of a covered building or contents loss and some of which are not. Many insureds probably fail to make claims that otherwise would be covered owing to the lack of knowledge that their policy covered such losses. These additional coverages are extensive, covering the better part of four pages in the ISO HO 2 and HO 3 policies, and include the following.

Debris Removal

The policy's coverage includes the costs of removing debris of covered property resulting from a loss caused by an insured peril. The debris removal coverage also applies to costs of removal of volcanic ash, dust, or particles from a volcanic eruption that has caused a direct physical loss to covered buildings or contents.

Debris removal expenses are included within the policy limits unless the total damage equals or exceeds the policy limits. In that case, the policy will pay debris removal expenses in addition to the policy limit, subject to the maximum of 5% of the limit applicable to the damaged property.

The debris removal coverage also extends to the costs of removal of the insured's downed trees felled by windstorm, hail, weight of ice, snow, or sleet and neighbors' trees felled by one of the policy's named perils, if one of two circumstances exist:

1. the felled tree damages a covered structure or
2. the felled tree blocks a driveway, handicapped access ramp, or fixture.

This coverage is subject to a maximum of $1,000 for any one loss and a $500 maximum for the removal of any one tree. These amounts are payable in addition to the policy limit.

Reasonable Repairs

The heading for this category of additional coverages is not generally descriptive. These are really two distinct coverages. First, the policy covers the reasonable costs incurred by the insured to protect covered property that has been damaged by a covered peril from further damage.

Second, if the measures taken by the insured to prevent further damage also involve repair costs, those repair costs will be covered. Again, the property in question must be covered property and the damage must have been caused by a covered cause of loss.

Neither of these coverages increases the policy limit applicable to the damaged covered property. Nor do these provisions relieve the insured of any of his or her duties stated in the policy's conditions, which include keeping accurate records of expenses, including repair expenses.

Trees, Shrubs, and Other Plants

The standard ISO HO 2 and HO 3 policies also provide up to 5% of the dwelling policy limit for loss to trees, shrubs, plants, or lawns at the residence premises caused by the perils of:

- fire or lightning;
- explosion;
- riot or civil commotion;
- aircraft;
- vehicles not owned or operated by residents of the residence premises;
- vandalism and malicious mischief; or,
- theft.

This coverage is in addition to the dwelling policy limit and is subject to a maximum of $500 for any one tree, shrub, or plant.

Fire Department Service Charge

This additional coverage applies up to $500 for fire department service charges that the insured has assumed under contract. Covered fire department service charges must be incurred when the fire department is called on to save or protect covered property from a covered peril. No fire department service charges are payable if the insured property is located within the limits of the city of fire protection district furnishing the response. When this additional coverage applies, it is payable in addition to the policy limit and without application of a deductible.

Credit Card, Forgery, and Counterfeit Money

With the rise in identity theft, this additional coverage is one more policyholders should be aware of. Under this coverage, the insurer will pay up to $500 for the legal obligation of an insured to pay because of the theft or unauthorized use of credit cards or electronic fund transfer (EFT) cards issued to or registered in an insured's name. This coverage is subject to limitations. In addition, it obligates the insurer to provide the insured with a legal defense in the event the insured is sued to collect the charges incurred by the unauthorized user. This additional coverage also applies to loss caused by forgery or alteration of any check or other negotiable instrument and by an insured's good faith acceptance of counterfeit United States or Canadian currency. This coverage is an addition to the policy limit and applies without a deductible.

The following restrictions apply—no coverage exists for use of a credit card, electronic fund transfer card, or access device:

- by a resident of a named insured's household;
- by any person who an insured entrusts with a credit card or EFT card or device; or,
- if an insured has not complied with all the terms and conditions under which the cards or devices are issued (such as, for example, disclosing personal identification members to others).

In addition, this coverage does not apply to loss arising out of business use or to loss arising out of dishonesty by an insured.

Loss Assessment

Loss assessment coverage can be important to insureds who are members of a homeowners association or cooperative association and potentially subject to assessments for the costs of repairs to common areas that are jointly owned by all the members of the association. This could occur, for example, if the homeowners association's own policy limits were not sufficient to repair or replace the damaged common area property. The insurer will pay up to $1,000 per loss (regardless of the number of assessments) for the insured's share of a loss assessment that results from direct loss to common property of a type that would have been a covered peril (excluding earthquake and land tremors before or after a volcanic eruption). This coverage only applies to assessments by the homeowners association against the members of the homeowners association. This additional coverage does not apply to assessments imposed by any governmental body or agency.

A single deductible applies per unit owned by an insured. This coverage is in addition to the policy limit.

Collapse

The collapse coverage of the current ISO HO 2 and HO 3 policies has been redrafted in an attempt to address a legal debate that has existed as to whether the *collapse* coverage required an actual falling down or caving in of all or part of the building or whether an *imminent* collapse was sufficient to trigger coverage. The current edition of the ISO HO 2 and HO 3 policies contains clarifications intended to make clear that an *actual* collapse is required for collapse coverage to apply.

The collapse coverage begins with a series of four definitions that state what is and is not considered to be a collapse. These definitions state that:

1. collapse means an abrupt falling down or caving in of a building or any part of a building with the result that the building or part of current intended purpose;

2. a building or any part of a building that is in danger of falling down or caving in is not considered to be in a state of collapse;

3. a part of a building that is standing is not considered to be in a state of collapse even if it has separated from another part of the building; and,

4. building or any part of a building that is standing is not considered to be in a state of collapse even if it shows evidence of cracking, bulging, sagging, bending, leaning, settling, shrinkage, or expansion.

The insuring agreement of the collapse coverage next provides that coverage will exist only if the collapse was caused by one or more of the named perils applicable to the personal property coverage or five additional specified perils. These five additional specified perils include the following:

1. decay hidden from view, unless the presence of such decay is known to an insured prior to collapse;

2. insect or vermin damage (*i.e.,* termite) that is hidden from view, unless the presence of such damage is known to an insured prior to collapse;
3. weight of contents, equipment, animals, or people;
4. weight of rain that collects on a roof; and,
5. use of defective materials or methods in construction, remodeling, or renovation if the collapse occurs during the course of the construction, remodeling, or renovation.

Finally, if the cause of the collapse is one of the five specified perils, the collapse coverage provisions state that collapse coverage does not apply to:

◆ awnings;
◆ fences;
◆ patios;
◆ decks;
◆ pavements;
◆ swimming pools;
◆ underground pipes;
◆ flues;
◆ drains;
◆ cesspools;
◆ septic tanks;
◆ foundations;
◆ retaining walls;
◆ bulkheads;
◆ piers;
◆ wharves; or,
◆ docks.

This is unless the loss to these categories of property is the direct result of the collapse of all or a part of a building.

The inclusion of collapse coverage in the policy does not operate to increase the policy limits.

Glass or Safety Glazing Material

This provision affords coverage for glass breakage that is caused directly by earth movement and also extends to direct physical loss to property that is caused by the glass fragments. For purposes of this coverage, glass means glass or glazing material that is part of the building (*i.e.,* windows and sky-lights), storm doors, or storm windows. It does not include glass used in picture frames, mirrors, or glassware. No glass coverage, except as the result of earthquake or earth movement, exists if the building has been vacant for a period of sixty days prior to the date of loss. The glass coverage is included within the policy limit and is not in addition to the policy limit.

Landlords' Furnishings

The landlord's furnishing coverage affords a $2,500 per loss sublimit, within the personal property policy limits, for appliances, carpeting, and other household furnishings in apartments on the residence premises rented to others or held for rental to others. Protection from theft is not covered under this provision.

Ordinance or Law

This is an important coverage and one that the insured should check carefully with his or her agent, particularly with respect to the question of what form of replacement cost coverage the policy may provide. Many insurers have in the past experienced coverage disputes with policyholders over replacement cost policies. Often, these disputes have had their origins in the fact that the insured did not maintain policy limits consistent with increasing home values and increasing costs of labor and materials used in construction, rebuilding, and repair.

Further, as the result of various catastrophic kinds of losses stemming from hurricanes, tornadoes, major wildfires, and earthquakes, various governmental bodies have enacted building codes and other laws that have resulted in increased construction costs after a loss has occurred. Examples include prohibition of replacement of roofs with wood shake shingles and methods of construction intended to help resist the force of windstorms or earthquakes.

As the result of these combined factors, many homeowners insurers began modifying their replacement cost provisions and increased cost of construction provisions to include insurance-to-value requirements or eliminate so-called *guaranteed replacement cost* provisions. Often, these modifications to replacement cost coverage provisions have been implemented through endorsements and are not contained in the insurers' basic policy forms.

It therefore is crucial that you determine what form of replacement cost coverage, if any, is included in your policy. You must determine whether that coverage includes coverage for the costs of compliance with changed building code requirements, and if not, whether more complete coverage is available.

This additional coverage provides that the insured may use up to 10% of the dwelling policy limit for increased costs incurred due to the enforcement of ordinances or laws that require or regulate the construction, demolition, remodeling, renovation, or repair of the part of the covered dwelling or other structure that has been damaged by a covered peril. This coverage also extends to the costs of demolition and reconstruction of an undamaged part of the building if:

- such demolition is required by ordinance or law as a result of covered damage to another part of the dwelling or other structure or
- it is necessary to complete the remodeling or repair of covered damage to another part of the building.

The ordinance or law coverage does not extend to loss in value of a covered dwelling or other structure resulting from compliance with the requirements of any ordinance or law, nor to costs of compliance with any ordinance or law requiring the insured to test for, monitor, or clean up pollutants. The ordinance or law coverage applies in addition to the policy limits.

Grave Markers
Covering the personal property peril is a $5,000 sublimit applicable to grave markers, including mausoleums, whether on or off the residence premises.

Proprietary Homeowners Policy Forms

When it comes to additional coverages, the policies offered by insurers that use their own proprietary forms have additional coverages that are generally similar to the foregoing provisions of the ISO HO 2 and HO 3 homeowners policies. There is, however, more variation in these coverages from insurer to insurer than in any other portion of the policy. The variations include both the categories of property subject to limitation, as well as the limits of liability applicable to the limitations.

Some policies have no felled trees coverage. Others have more limited collapse coverage. Others do not include homeowners association loss assessment coverage, except as an optional coverage for a premium surcharge.

An important additional coverage included in some homeowners policies is sewer back-up coverage. This is often an excluded peril. It is a significant additional coverage that extends to loss caused by water that backs up through sewers and drains. Sewer backups can cause significant losses to both the structure and contents. When this coverage is included additionally, it is a significant broadening of coverage compared with what is afforded by the ISO HO 3 homeowners policy. In short, this is an area where comparison shopping based on coverages provided, rather than price, is well worth your time.

As stated, the additional coverages of homeowners policies can be extensive and complex, and include many coverages of which the average policyholder may not be fully aware. This section of your policy is worth taking a few minutes to review. It is also an area in which competitive price quotes can be highly misleading, unless you have specimen copies of the policies under consideration to review and compare.

Chapter 7
Exclusions

As previously noted, homeowners policies contain exclusions within the basic policy form. It is, however, necessary to review a homeowners policy's endorsements in order to determine whether any of the exclusions contained in the basic policy form have been modified or any new exclusions have been added to further restrict coverage. Often, when an exclusion contained in the basic policy form has been modified by an endorsement, it can be difficult to figure out what is or is not covered.

Before discussing the particular exclusions, a review of the language that begins the exclusions section needs to be discussed. The ISO HO 3 policy first states the broad all-risk insuring agreement and then begins its prefatory statement with respect to the exclusions. This language states the following.

- *We do not insure against risk of direct physical loss to property described in Coverages A and B.*
- *We do not insure, however, for loss:*
    a. Excluded under Section I—Exclusions.

SECTION 1 EXCLUSIONS

This introductory phrase refers the reader to the enumerated exclusions at Section I, which comprise twelve categories of exclusions, and which

e their own introductory language that is of great significance. This group
f exclusions is discussed first here.

The introductory language that precedes the exclusions listed in
Section I—Exclusions, states:

> *We do not insure for loss caused directly or indirectly by any of the*
> *following. Such loss is excluded regardless of any other cause or event*
> *contributing concurrently or in any sequence to the loss. These exclu-*
> *sions apply whether or not the loss event results in widespread damage*
> *or affects a substantial area.*

The problem this language attempts to address is that of multiple causes
of loss, in which some causes are covered causes of loss and others are not.
This is referred to in insurance parlance as *multiple causation* or *concurrent causation*. The language just quoted states that if any excluded cause of loss is
involved in a given loss, no coverage exists.

Despite the existence of this type of policy language—often referred to as
anticoncurrent causation language—coverage disputes continue to arise in the
multiple or concurrent causation context. Courts in the United States have
taken a variety of approaches to the issue of multiple causation. The efficient
proximate cause standard is by far the approach taken in the majority of jurisdictions in the United States.

This efficient proximate causation analysis seeks to discern what the predominant cause of loss is. It may not necessarily be the first cause in the
sequence of events leading to the loss, although looking at the *triggering* cause
of loss is frequently a useful analysis. Also, the efficient proximate cause of
loss may well not be the immediate cause of loss (the last to occur), although
again, that is something that needs to be considered in reaching a reasoned
conclusion as to what, in fact, is the predominating cause of loss.

Under this efficient proximate cause of loss analysis, if the predominant
cause of loss is covered, the loss is covered. The converse is true as well. If the
predominant cause of loss is an excluded peril, no coverage exists. Often, the
result of this analysis may be that there are actually multiple losses, each of
which requires its own efficient proximate cause analysis.

Questions arising from the issue of the enforceability of anticoncurrent causation language are likely to remain the subject of dispute between insurers and policyholders for the foreseeable future.

The exclusions of the ISO HO 3 homeowners policy appear in the following order in the policy.

Ordinance or Law

This exclusion precludes coverage for three categories of loss. First, it applies to loss from enforcement of ordinances or laws requiring or regulating the construction, demolition, remodeling, renovation, or repair of property, including removal of resulting debris. Now, I know this is confusing—we just went through similar language in the discussion of the additional coverages. Well, the statement of this exclusion is followed by an exception for that amount of coverage that is provided for such losses in the additional coverages parallel section of the policy. Why would the drafter of a policy set things up this way? It is done to assure that when there is a limited amount of coverage afforded for a particular risk, it is made clear that such limited coverage as may be available for that risk is all the coverage that applies to the loss.

Further, the final paragraph of the ordinance or law exclusion states that the ordinance or law exclusion applies whether or not the property has been physically damaged. The additional coverage "ordinance or law" coverage exists when there has been a covered physical loss to at least part of the insured premises. Governmental bodies also enact ordinances or laws affecting property owners, the enforcement of which is not dependent on the occurrence of a covered loss. For example, there are commonly ordinances that require minimum set-backs of structures from streets, sidewalks, or adjoining buildings. If your house is in violation of the set-back requirement and you are ordered to remove that portion, you will not be covered. That is why that exclusion is there, and why it has been written to interact with the limited ordinance or law coverage afforded under the additional coverage section.

Second, no coverage exists for the operation of ordinances or laws that result in the loss of value to property. This can occur when areas around your property are rezoned, resulting in the value of your property decreasing. (Nobody wants the park at the end of the block turned into a cement factory.) An economic loss in the absence of direct physical loss is not the intended subject of the type of policy in question and no coverage exists for this loss of value.

Third, the ordinance or law exclusion precludes coverage for loss arising from laws addressing environmental pollution issues. You do not have to have caused any environmental pollution to become a defendant in a pollution clean-up action. Once you are in the *chain of title* of a contaminated property, you are potentially on the hook under federal and state environmental pollution laws for the cost of *remediation* (cleaning up) of those pollutants. Your homeowners insurer provides no coverage for the costs of remediating pollution on your property, whether you are the person who caused the pollution or not.

Earth Movement

The earth movement exclusion is not limited to the peril of earthquake, but also includes:

- land shock waves, including tremors associated with volcanic eruptions;
- landslides, mudslides, and mudflow;
- subsidence or sinkholes; and,
- any other earth movement, including earth rising, sinking, or shifting (for example, due to variation or changes in the amount of subsurface water that causes soil to expand or contract).

This exclusion applies regardless of whether the earth movement is the product of natural, human, or animal forces, unless fire or explosion results from the earth movement. Fire and explosion are referred to as *ensuing losses*, for which coverage expressly exists.

Water Damage

Although coverage for accidental discharges or overflows of water from plumbing, air conditioning, sprinkler systems, or household appliances applies, there are many types of water damage beyond those categories. The water damage exclusions list those types of water damage that are not covered.

The flood category includes not only floods, but other similar (and often overlapping) concepts such as: surface water, waves, tidal water, overflow of a body of water, or spray from any of these, whether or not driven by wind. Policies will often contain repetitive listings of substantially similar concepts to avoid claims in which, for example, a homeowner may state a flood did not cause the damage but rather an overflow of water. The repetitive list is designed to cover these claims that seek to rely on trivial semantic distinctions to assert coverage for excluded perils.

Flood damage falls into the category of losses that are *too predictable* for insurance in the normal markets. Where floods have occurred, they will reoccur—it is only a matter of time. Flood plains are well-documented by the United States Army Corps of Engineers, including with historical records that permit a reasonable estimate of the frequency of flood in a given area. For coastal areas subject to hurricane flooding, similar information is available.

Because the peril of flood is universally excluded, the Federal Flood Insurance Program was established. If you are in a flood area, your agent or broker can help you obtain a separate flood insurance policy.

The second category of excluded water damage losses is water or water-borne material (*i.e.,* sewage) that backs-up through sewers or drains or which overflows or is discharged from sump pumps or related equipment. This is a long-standing exclusion that nonetheless comes to the unfortunate surprise of many policyholders each year. While such persons often have recourse against a governmental body or sewer/water agency in the event of such losses, the claims process against a governmental entity can be protracted and difficult. There is, however, something you can do to help prevent such losses. Consult a plumber. If your toilets and drain lines are not equipped with antiback-flow devices, get such devices installed.

The third category of excluded water-damage losses is subsurface water that causes damage by exerting pressure on or seeping or leaking through a building, sidewalk, driveway, foundation, swimming pool, or other structure. Problems of this nature are commonly the product of poor siting or construction. The policy excludes coverage for this category of damage because it will recur unless the fundamental problem that created it is corrected.

Finally, as with the earth movement exclusion, loss by fire, explosion, or theft that results from water damage is covered as an ensuing loss.

Power Failure

Under the ISO HO 3 policy, no coverage exists for power failure that originates away from the residence premises, unless such power failure results in a loss from a separate covered peril.

Neglect

Neglect is defined as the neglect of an insured to save and preserve property after the time of loss. When this exclusion applies, it should apply to preclude coverage for the amount of additional damage caused by the insured's neglect, unless the insured's neglect was the predominating or triggering cause of the loss in the first place.

War

The war risk exclusion has been a fixture of insurance policies for generations. In light of recent events, questions have arisen whether loss due to acts of terrorism are subject to the war risk exclusion. The answer is: probably not. One of the subparagraphs of the war risk exclusion provides that war includes: *undeclared war, civil war, insurrection, rebellion, or revolution.* Undeclared war connotes military action by a foreign nation and probably does not reasonably embrace the concept of acts of terrorism. Acts of civil war, insurrection, rebellion or revolution conceivably could embrace acts of domestic terrorism, but only when committed by organized groups.

Nuclear Hazard

This exclusion does no more than cross-reference another section that states that nuclear hazard is considered an uninsurable risk. The sole exception to this exclusion is direct loss by fire resulting from the nuclear hazard.

Intentional Loss

As a general concept, it should come as no surprise that a policy excludes loss arising out of any act an insured commits or conspires to commit with the intent to cause a loss. What may come as a surprise is that in the second paragraph of this exclusion, the policy provides that an intentional loss committed by *any* insured will result in the preclusion in coverage for all insureds. This precludes a so-called *innocent co-insured* from coverage when another insured commits an intentional loss. While the courts of the fifty states are split on this issue, the majority of jurisdictions hold that no coverage exists for innocent co-insureds for intentional acts of another insured.

Governmental Action

This exclusion precludes coverage for the destruction, confiscation, or seizure of a dwelling, other structures, or personal property by order of any governmental or public authority. There is a significant exception to this exclusion. When a governmental body acts at the time of a fire to prevent its spread, loss will be covered.

In practical terms, this exclusion prevents coverage when a government seizes property based on the arrest or conviction for certain crimes or offenses, such as drug related offenses.

Section 1: Concurrent Causation

The second group of exclusions applicable to the property coverages of homeowners policies consists of three categories that are of great importance. However, unlike the preceding nine exclusions, this group of three categories of exclusions is not made subject to the *anticoncurrent causation* language. Effectively, these exclusions are narrower than those we have just discussed.

There are a couple additional qualifications to note. First, these exclusions only apply to the dwelling and other structures coverages, not to the contents coverage. This further narrows the scope of these exclusions.

Second, if there is an ensuing loss to the dwelling or other structures by a covered peril for which coverage is not precluded by any other policy provision, that ensuing loss is covered.

Weather Conditions

This exclusion has a substantial qualification and is actually relatively narrow. This exclusion only applies if weather conditions contribute in any way with a cause of loss or an event excluded in any of the exclusions previously discussed to produce the loss. Let's try some illustrative examples. Weather conditions cause a power failure, resulting in loss to contents of refrigerators and freezers. The exclusion applies. Heavy rain causes a hillside to give way, resulting in a mudslide that damages your house or garage. The exclusion applies. Lighting causes a power failure that causes a sump pump to cease operating, resulting in backup or overflow of the sump. The exclusion applies.

Acts or Decisions

The language of this exclusion tends to strike the average reader as, alternatively, nebulous or opaque. It states:

> *We do not insure for loss to property described in Coverages A or B caused by any of the following...*
>
> > *Acts or decisions, including the failure to act or decide, of any person, group, organization or governmental body.*

The nebulous nature of this exclusion is underscored that there is little, if any, case law interpreting it. Thus, whether it would apply to a particular claim would depend on the facts of the claim and the plain language of the exclusion. As a practical matter, when a policy provision has not been construed by courts, insurers are often reluctant to rely on such a provision as the basis for a denial of coverage, unless the insurer has other and stronger defenses to a claim.

Faulty, Inadequate, or Defective Maintenance or Construction

This is the most important of the three categories of exclusions. The essential theme of this category is that coverage does not apply to losses that are the result of poor design, planning, siting, construction, materials, or maintenance. The message communicated by this exclusion is two-fold. First, if another person or third party causes the loss, the insured's remedy is to sue them, not to look to his or her own property insurance.

Second, if the cause of loss is the insured's own failure to maintain his or her property—too bad. This body of exclusions puts the burden on the insured not only to maintain his or her property to assure the existence of coverage, but also to take due care in assessing the quality of property before purchase and the competence of persons with whom the insured contracts to perform remodeling or reconstruction. This would also exclude problems developing from do-it-yourself remodeling or construction projects where loss results from defective design, materials, or construction.

Under this exclusion lie four subcategories. The first precludes coverage for faulty, inadequate, or defective *planning, zoning, development, surveying, or siting*. In other words, the subcategory precludes coverage for errors by governmental bodies, real estate developers, and design professionals such as geologists, soils engineers, and architects. The purpose of this exclusion is to cause losses of this nature to be borne by the party whose errors or misjudgments are the cause of loss.

Problems that would fall under this exclusion could take years to develop, leaving the insured seemingly without remedy against the party at fault due to statutes of limitations. However, under the *ensuing loss* clause, if the nature of the damage caused by this category of exclusions is covered, coverage will exists. For example, a soils engineer's failure to identify an ancient landslide results in subsidence damage, no coverage exists. If there is subsidence damage that ruptures a gas line and the dwelling is destroyed by a fire, coverage would then exist.

The second of the four subcategories of this exclusions precludes coverage for *faulty, inadequate, or defective...design, specifications, workmanship, repair, construction, renovation, remodeling, grading, or compaction*. There is some obvious overlap with this group of exclusions with the previous group, particularly with respect to design and specifications. This group of exclusions goes more to loss caused by age than the actual construction of the dwelling. Notably, this exclusion applies not only to loss arising from defective original construction, but also defective repair, remodeling, and renovation.

The presence of this exclusion is the reason to choose remodeling or repair contractors carefully, and to take care that if you do your own remodeling or repair work, it is done correctly and in compliance with building codes. The ensuing loss clause again provides an exception to this group of exclusions for ensuing loss by a covered peril. However, merely defective work will not result in coverage.

The third subcategory of these exclusions precludes coverage for faulty, inadequate, or defective, *materials used in repair, construction, renovation or remodeling.* There is some overlap between this subcategory and the previous subcategory. This exclusion focuses on loss caused by improperly chosen or defective materials, as opposed to defective performance of the work. The ensuing loss clause restores coverage for loss within this exclusion for ensuing losses that are caused by covered perils.

The fourth and final subcategory of this group of exclusions is for loss resulting from faulty, inadequate, or defective *maintenance of part or all of any property whether on or off the residence premises.* The ensuing loss coverage will restore coverage for ensuing losses caused by covered perils.

ADDITIONAL EXCLUSIONS

The next group of exclusions in the ISO HO 2 and HO 3 is essentially the flip side of several of the exceptions to certain of the personal property named perils, and/or of certain of the Additional Coverages.

Collapse

The first of these exclusions is for loss involving *collapse*, except as is provided in the *Additional Coverages* peril of collapse. As discussed, the collapse coverage is essentially a named perils coverage, which, under the ISO HO 2 and HO 3 policies, requires an actual collapse of the building or parts of the building for coverage to arise. This collapse exclusion is also modified by an ensuing loss clause that provides that coverage exists for loss ensuing from an otherwise noncovered collapse if that ensuing loss is caused by a covered peril.

Freezing

The second of these exclusions is for freezing of a plumbing, heating, air conditioning, fire sprinkler system, household appliance or for discharge, leakage, or overflow from within the system or appliance caused by freezing. There are exceptions to this exclusion. This exclusion does not apply if the insured has used reasonable care to maintain heat in the building or has shut off and drained the water from the system or appliance. As with the personal property named peril, plumbing systems and household appliances are defined as not including sump pumps or related equipment, roof drains, gutters, downspouts or similar fixtures or equipment. This is an example of an exclusion that is essentially the flip side of one of the personal property coverage named perils. Thus, the scope of coverage for the peril of *freezing* is essentially the same for the dwelling and other structures as it is for personal property.

Freezing and Thawing

The next exclusion precludes coverage for freezing, thawing, pressure, or weight of water or ice whether driven by wind or not to four categories of property:

- fences, pavements, patios, or swimming pools;
- footings, foundations, bulkheads, walls, or any other structure or device that supports all or part of the building or other structure;
- retaining walls or bulkheads that do not support all or part of the building or other structures; and,
- piers, wharves, or docks. (This exclusion also has some parallels to the subsurface waters portion of the water damage exclusion.)

Theft of Construction Materials

The next exclusion in this group is for theft of construction materials and supplies from a dwelling under construction until the dwelling is finished and occupied. This exclusion is parallel to one of the exceptions to the personal property named peril of theft.

Vandalism and Malicious Mischief

The next exclusion is for loss caused by vandalism and malicious mischief, but only if the dwelling has been vacant for sixty or more consecutive days before the loss. This exclusion does not apply to dwellings in the course of construction.

Repeated Seepage or Leakage of Water

The next exclusion is for loss caused by constant or repeated seepage or leakage of water or steam over a period of weeks, months, or years from within a plumbing, heating, air conditioning, fire sprinkler system, or household appliance. This is a more specific example of the faulty, inadequate, or defective maintenance and neglect exclusions. As made clear by the personal property coverage named perils, coverage exists if the personal property caused by accidental discharges of water from such systems, including those caused by freezing. Further, the freezing exclusion applicable to the dwelling and other structure coverages has exceptions that will permit some coverage. The point here is that it is the insured's duty to maintain his or her property and to take reasonable steps to protect it from loss. Failure to correct such leaks over a period of weeks, months, and years renders such water damage nonaccidental, nonfortuitous, and hence, not covered.

Mold, Fungus, or Wet Rot

The next exclusion in this group is for loss caused by mold, fungus, or wet rot. As with personal property coverage, if the mold, fungus, or wet rot damage results from an accidental discharge and is not apparent to the insured because it is hidden, coverage will exist. This exclusion therefore is parallel to and consistent with the constant or repeated water leakage exclusion, as mold, fungus, or wet rot resulting from such constant or repeated water leakage is not covered.

Exclusions Subject to an Ensuing Loss Clause

The next group of exclusions is unified by a lengthy exception that is essentially parallel to the personal property accidental water discharge named perils. These exclusions are subject to an ensuing loss clause. These exclusions are:

- ◆ wear and tear, marring, and deterioration, which are all examples of expected, nonfortuitous losses;
- ◆ mechanical breakdown, latent defect, inherent vice, or any other quality in property that causes it to damage or destroy itself

(parallels the faulty, inadequate, or defective materials used in construction exclusion);

◆ smog, rust, dry rot, or other corrosion (parallels the maintenance exclusion);

◆ smoke from agricultural smudging or industrial operations (corresponds with the exception to the personal property named perils coverage for smoke);

◆ discharge of pollutants, unless the release of pollutants is caused by one of the personal property coverage named perils (*pollutants* is specifically and quite broadly defined in the policy);

◆ settling, shrinking, bulging, or expansion, including resulting cracking of bulkheads, pavements, patios, footings, foundations, walls, floors, roofs, or ceilings (this exclusion dovetails with the earth movement, subsurface water damage, freezing, and collapse exclusions);

◆ birds, vermin, rodents, or insects (which include termites). These exclusions are specific examples of failure to maintain; and,

◆ animals owned or kept by an insured.

COMPARISON SHOPPING

The exclusions of homeowners policies are another area in which comparison shopping may help you make an informed choice of insurer. Homeowners insurance policies may vary widely in terms of how particular exclusions are worded or exceptions to exclusions are worded that have the practical effect of providing broader coverage. The subject of exclusions is one in which homeowners insurers seek to compete with each other, although their competition is often not very transparent to the insurance consumer. It often requires actual comparison of specimen policy forms from various insurers to discern the differences in the scope of exclusions. Unfortunately, some insurers will not give out specimen copies of their policies and too few consumers take the time to ask for them.

EXCLUSIONS ADDED BY OTHER INSURERS

Some insurers' policies add exclusions not contained in the ISO HO 2 and HO 3 policies. For example, a relatively common exclusion precludes coverage for loss resulting from an increase in hazard at the insured premises that is within the knowledge or control of an insured. A methamphetamine lab is an example of one extreme. Such activities are criminal in nature and involve the use of highly flammable and explosive chemicals. Failing to replace broken or nonfunctioning door locks is another example—failing to secure premises renders them more vulnerable to theft and vandalism losses.

Under the law of most states, where an exclusion of this nature refers to *knowledge or control of an insured*, the knowledge or control of *any* insured will have the effect of defeating coverage for other insureds who did not have knowledge of or control over the increase in hazard that leads to loss.

Water damage exclusions also vary from insurer to insurer. The ISO policies exclude coverage for sewer back-up losses. Some insurers' water damage exclusions do not exclude coverage for sewer back-up losses. If your house is situated where it may be subject to such losses, this is an issue that is worth spending your time to inquire whether coverage is available from an insurer at a premium that fits your budget.

Another point to consider when you are comparing policy forms from various insurers is to examine *ensuing loss* clauses that are part of exclusions. Ensuing loss clauses are exceptions to exclusions. Some ensuing loss clauses limit coverage to ensuing fire or explosion. Other ensuing loss clauses extend coverage to ensuing loss caused by any covered cause of loss. And, of course, there are examples between these two extremes.

Chapter 8
Conditions

Policy conditions address issues such as the insured's duties in the event of loss or how claims are valued and settled. They also provide for mechanisms for resolution of disagreements between the insured and the insurer over the amount of the loss. Many of the conditions applicable to the property coverages have their origins in whatever form of standard fire policy is deemed to be part of your homeowners policy as a matter of law of the state where you reside.

Conditions are divided into two sections. First there is the group of conditions that applies only to the property coverages. Second, there is a group of conditions that applies generally to all coverages, both property and liability. Each group will be addressed.

CONDITIONS APPLICABLE TO PROPERTY COVERAGES

The first condition is entitled *Insurable Interest and Limits of Liability.* This condition provides that regardless of whether more than one person has an insurable interest in covered property, the insurer will not be liable in any one loss to any insured for more than that insured's pecuniary interest in the property as of the time of loss. This condition also provides that the insurer will not be liable in any one loss more than the limit of liability or policy limit that applies to the item of property in question.

DUTIES AFTER LOSS

This is an extensive group of conditions comprising eight sections, that further encompass thirteen subparagraphs. All of these are highly important policy provisions standard to all homeowners policies and merit your attention.

The introductory paragraph to this section states that the insurer has no duty to provide coverage for an otherwise covered loss if the insurer is prejudiced by the failure of the named insured, another insured, or a representative of an insured, to comply with the list of duties that follows.

- ◆ Give the insurer or the insurer's agent prompt notice of the loss.
- ◆ Notify the police in the event of a theft loss.
- ◆ Give the issuer of a credit card, electronic fund transfer card, or access device notice of loss or of unauthorized use of same as required by the provisions of the agreement between the issuer and the insured.
- ◆ Protect the property from further damage. If repairs to property are required, the insured must:
  - ■ make reasonable and necessary repairs to protect the property and
  - ■ keep an accurate account of repair expenses.
- ◆ Cooperate with your insurer in its investigation of the claim. This means returning phone calls and responding to correspondence promptly. If you do not understand what a communication or an information request from your insurer means or why it is important, promptly call the claim representative or your agent and ask for an explanation so that you can provide an appropriate response. Any delay on your part that reflects mere silence in response to an insurer's request for information (in appropriate cases) can be taken as evidence of a failure to cooperate.
- ◆ Prepare an inventory of damaged personal property which shows:
  - ■ the quantity;
  - ■ the description;
  - ■ the actual cash value; and,
  - ■ the amount of loss of all items for which loss is claimed.

You must attach all bills, receipts, and related documents that justify or support the figures shown in the inventory. This can potentially be a gargantuan task in the event of a sizeable loss. Most people can recall reasonably well what items have been damaged, lost, or destroyed so that the quantity and description portions of the inventory are likely to be easier to prepare. Areas that can be problematic here are where the insured may have extensive collections of books, or audio recordings. Other items, such as furniture that has been passed along through a family with no clear record of the value or acquisition cost, can also be problematic. The valuation issues can be even more difficult—few of us retain the receipts for everything we buy.

The requirement that the insured submit an inventory of the damaged, destroyed, or lost property is one of the reasons that it is frequently suggested that insureds videotape or photograph the interior of their homes with closets and cabinets open from time to time. This will create at least a partial visual record of their belongings and that videotape or set of photographs should be stored in a safe place, such as a safe deposit box.

◆ Allow the insurer to examine the insured property as often as the insurer reasonably requests; provide the insurer with records and documents upon its request and permit the insurer to make copies; submit to an examination under oath, outside the presence of any other insured; and, sign a transcript of the examination under oath. Examinations under oath are often, but not always, requested by insurers in cases in which the insurer perceives the insured to be uncooperative with the investigation of the claim. Examinations can also be requested when there are aspects of the claim that suggest that there may be a fraudulent aspect to the claim. Refusal to submit to an examination under oath can afford the insurer a basis for refusing to pay a claim in its entirety.

The examination is conducted before a court reporter, who takes down all the questions and answers, and transcribes them into a booklet form after the examination has concluded. The person who conducts the examination is usually a lawyer retained by the insurer. Under the laws of most states, the insured who is being questioned has the right to be represented by counsel at his or her own expense at the examination. The degree to which the insured's lawyer can object to questions varies from state to state. Usually, when an insurer demands an examination under oath it also demands a lengthy list of documents for the insured to produce for inspection and copying at the examination. These document inspection requests in conjunction with examinations under oath can be duplicative of previous demands by the insurer, which is the insurer's prerogative.

Due to concerns that some insurers exercise their rights to demand an examination under oath unreasonably, some states have enacted some restrictions. For example, the California Insurance Code now provides that insurers may conduct an examination under oath only to obtain information that is relative to and reasonably necessary to process or investigate the claim. This, however, is a rather nebulous standard. Examinations under oath may be conducted only on reasonable notice, at a reasonably convenient place, and for a reasonable period of time. The insured has the right to have counsel present, who can assert any objection to a question that would be permissible in a deposition under state or federal law. The insurer must provide the insured with a free copy of the transcript of the examination under oath after it is transcribed and must permit the insured to make sworn corrections to the transcript.

◆ Meet the proof of loss requirements that are preconditions to claim payment by the insurer.

The signed and sworn proof of loss must be submitted to the insurer by the insured within sixty days of the insurer's request. It is common for the insurer and the insured to agree to extensions of the sixty-day deadline for submission of the proof of loss. You should confirm any such agreement in writing. The proof of loss must set forth, to the best of your knowledge and belief, the following information:

- the time and cause of loss;
- the interest of all insureds, all others on the property involved, and all liens on the property;
- any other insurance that may cover the loss;
- any changes in the title to or occupancy of the property during the term of the policy;
- specifications of damaged buildings and detailed repair estimates;
- the inventory of damaged, destroyed, or lost (in the case of theft) personal property;
- receipts for any additional living expenses incurred and records that support the fair rental value loss if a claim is being made for same; and,
- evidence or an affidavit that supports a claim under the credit card electronic fund transfer card coverage, stating the amount and cause of loss, if such a loss is being claimed.

LOSS SETTLEMENT

The loss settlement conditions of the property coverages of homeowners policies comprise an area where the policies of various insurers are likely to substantially differ. Thus, a somewhat more generic discussion is appropriate. The issues that arise under the loss settlement conditions involve the collision of and interaction between a number of concepts and policy provisions, including:

- policy limits;
- the concept of insurance-to-value and the effect of your failure to maintain sufficient insurance-to-value;
- the concept of actual cash value;
- the different forms of replacement costs coverage;
- the concept of increased costs of construction or repair due to the operation of new or different building code requirements or other such laws; and,
- the concept of repair or replacement with like kind and quality along with the related concept of *betterment.*

POLICY LIMITS AND INSURANCE-TO-VALUE

The availability of coverage for dwellings and other structures is crucially dependent on the concept of insurance-to-value. The policy limits for these coverages are stated in the policy's declarations. Choosing adequate policy limits is a crucial decision. Adequate insurance-to-value is a precondition to the availability of any of the varying forms of replacement cost coverage as may exist or nominally be provided for in your policy.

No one should consider insuring only to actual cash value. Insuring to actual cash value makes it a virtual certainty that you will have only partial coverage in the event of a loss. In the event of a moderate loss, insuring only to actual cash value could make the difference between being able to repair your home and replace your contents and being forced to abandon your house.

The concept of adequate insurance-to-value is another reason why your agent's knowledge and expertise is crucial. He or she needs to be up to date on current construction and materials costs. All insurers and their agents rely on regionally adjusted construction costs guides for recommending and setting dwelling policy limits. Some of these guides are better, more realistic, and more current than others.

You need to be able to describe your home to an agent when seeking a quote accurately—that includes square footage; number of stories, when built, type of construction (frame, stucco, brick); type and age of roof; type of electrical and plumbing systems; type of furnace and water heaters; etc. The list goes on, including any special or unusual features that apply to the home. These can include such things as decks, awnings, swimming pools, patios, canopies, and unusual masonry or stonework.

This is especially important if you have unusual separate structures whose values are likely to exceed the standard policy limits provided. Many insurers arbitrarily set the policy limit for separate structures at only 10% of the dwelling limit. If you have a guesthouse or other unusual, higher than normal value, separate structure on your premises, you need to provide the agent with as much detail about that structure as you do for your main house. Similar comments apply to a garage with a finished space such as a bedroom, office, or studio or a photographic darkroom.

Tell your agent everything about your home and property's features that you do not want to have to spend your own money on to repair or replace if your policy limits turn out to be inadequate to cover a loss. Do everything you can to avoid under-insuring—assure that you have sufficient insurance-to-value. You are far better off over-estimating necessary policy limits rather than underestimating them. You are probably going to need to do some homework and will potentially need to be a little bit pushy to assure adequate insurance-to-value. A failure to maintain policy limits at a level sufficient to qualify for whatever form of replacement cost coverage your policy provides can have the result that your loss will be covered only on an actual cash value basis.

When it comes to your home, you cannot really rely on real estate values as an indicator of actual cash value for insurance purposes, because the sale price of real estate includes the value of land and does not necessarily reflect construction costs. That's why understanding what construction costs are or can be is so crucial to the concept of insurance-to-value.

Each insurer defines replacement cost differently. There are six general categories of coverage for disclosure purposes as to the different forms of replacement cost coverage. From these general categories you can develop the right kinds of questions to learn what levels of coverage your insurer offers, what policy limits you need to carry to qualify for each level of coverage, and thereby to determine whether you want to seek alternative quotes for differing from other insurers.

First, there is actual cash value coverage (*i.e.*, coverage for the fair market value of the dwelling at the time of loss, up to the policy limit). This can be stated ultimately as the cost of replacing or repairing the damaged or destroyed dwelling with like or equivalent construction, up to the policy limit.

Second, there is building code upgrade coverage. This covers the additional costs, up to stated limits, to repair or replace a damaged or destroyed dwelling to conform to current building codes as of the time of loss or rebuilding.

Third, there is replacement cost coverage. This covers the cost to repair or replace the damaged or destroyed dwelling with like or equivalent construction, up to the policy limit. In addition, most replacement cost policies require that you actually repair or replace the damaged or destroyed dwelling to recover on a replacement cost basis, with loss payable only on an actual cash value basis until repair or replacement is complete. Replacement cost coverage of this type requires that you insure your dwelling to at least 80% of its replacement cost as of the time of loss.

Fourth, there is extended replacement cost coverage—that is, the cost to repair or replace the damaged or destroyed dwelling with like or equivalent construction, subject to a specified additional percentage over the dwelling limit of liability. This specified percentage can very widely from insurer to insurer. You need to check.

Most extended replacement cost coverages require that the insured carry policy limits equal to the full replacement cost at the time of policy issuance, not at the time of loss, and to agree to periodic increases in the policy limit to adjust for inflation. Such coverages also require the insured to permit your dwelling to be inspected by the insurer and to require you to notify the insurer of any improvements that increase the value of the dwelling by a specified percent. As with replacement cost policies, most extended replacement cost policies require repair or replacement in full before a replacement cost recovery will be paid by the insurer.

Fifth, there is guaranteed replacement cost without regard to policy limits with limited or no building cost upgrade coverage. This variant of replacement cost coverage will pay the full amount required to repair or replace the damaged or destroyed dwelling with like or equivalent construction regardless of policy limits, but does not include all additional costs of repair or replacement of the dwelling to comply with new building statutes in effect at the time of rebuilding. To qualify for this form of coverage, you must insure the dwelling to its full replacement cost at the time of policy issuance, must accept periodic increases in the policy limit to adjust for inflation, and must permit the insurer to inspect the property. Finally, you must notify your insurer of any alterations that increase the value of the dwelling by a specified percentage in the policy.

Sixth, there is guaranteed replacement cost with full building code upgrade coverage. This form of replacement cost coverage pays the full amount to repair or replace the damaged or destroyed dwelling with like or equivalent construction regardless of policy limits, including all increased costs of construction caused by new or different building statutes. The same preconditions for coverage apply: full insurance to value; acceptance of periodic increases in policy limits; permitting the insurer to inspect; and, notification of increases in value due to alterations that exceed a minimum percent specified in the policy.

A particular insurer may not offer all of these variations, regardless of your willingness to pay increased premiums for a particular form of coverage. This, again, is the situation where an independent agent may have an advantage over a captive agent that represents only one insurer. An independent agent may have access to insurers willing to quote and write the form of replacement cost coverage you desire that a direct writing agent may not be able to provide.

Having accurately calculated the replacement cost to their home and provided the percent of additional coverage in excess of policy limits for which coverage is included if sufficient, most people can do fine with a policy that includes *both* extended replacement cost coverage *and* building code upgrade coverage. If your policy limit is set at a sufficiently high level, extended replacement cost coverage not including building code upgrade coverage *may* be sufficient. If you choose this alternative, you will need to do a very good job of calculating the costs of reconstructing your home.

NOTE: *All forms of replacement cost coverage are stated in terms of repair or replacement with like or equivalent construction. If you decide that you want to make improvements as part of the repair or replacement of your damaged dwelling, the costs of improved materials or fixtures is not covered. Replacement cost coverage is intended to put you back in the same position you were in before loss, not in a better position.*

If your policy limits fall below a certain percent of the dwelling's replacement cost at the time of loss—usually 80%—the amount you recover may be reduced. Often, homeowners policies contain provisions that allow for recovery only in the proportion that your policy limits bear to 80% of the replacement cost of the dwelling. For example, the value of your home is $500,000, but your policy has a dwelling policy limit of only 60% of the replacement cost ($300,000). Eighty percent of your dwelling's replacement cost is $400,000 ($500,000 x 80% = $400,000). $300,000 divided by $400,000 equals 75%. Therefore, after applying your deductible, you would be entitled to recover only 75% of the amount of your loss subject to the policy limit. In the event of a total loss, you would only be able to recover 75% of $300,000, or $225,000.

As you can see, the potential financial consequences of not maintaining sufficient insurance-to-value can be severe. Consult with your agent regularly to ensure that your policy limits are sufficient. When you consult with your agent about the sufficiency of your policy limits, document his or her advice as to the amount of recommended coverage. If you later have a loss and the insurer determines that you were not insured-to-value, you have created a basis for:

- ◆ requesting that the insurer retroactively increase your policy limit on the grounds that you relied on the advice of its agent in setting your policy limit or
- ◆ an errors or omissions claim against your agent based on the improper advice as to your policy limit that caused a partially uninsured loss.

LOSS TO A PAIR OR SET

This condition gives the insurer two alternatives in the event of a loss to a pair or set of personal property items. The insurer may:

1. repair or replace any part to replace the pair or set to its preloss value or
2. pay the difference between the actual cash value of the property before and after the loss.

APPRAISAL

Appraisal can be invoked to determine the amount of loss. Such disputes might involve the valuation of items of damaged or destroyed personal property or involve the dispute over what constitutes like or equivalent construction.

Either the insurer or the insured may demand appraisal of a loss. If appraisal is demanded, each party chooses an appraiser—who the policy says should be competent and impartial—within twenty days after receiving a written request from the other party to submit the claim to appraisal. The two party-designated appraisers are to choose an umpire. If the party appraisers cannot agree on the umpire, either party may apply to a judge in a court of record in the state where the residence premises are located to choose the umpire.

The party appraisers then state the amount of the loss. If, on comparison of the party appraisers' respective loss valuation, they are in agreement, that is the amount of loss payable. If the appraisers differ as to their respective valuations of the amount of loss, they are to submit their differences to the umpire. A loss valuation agreed to by the umpire and one of the two party appraisers will determine the amount of loss.

The appraisal condition provides that each party will:

- pay its own appraiser and
- share the expenses of the appraisal and the umpire equally. (This can result in significant costs to the insured in certain circumstances.)

The appraisal condition is designed to be quick, relatively informal, relatively inexpensive, and self-executing (*i.e.,* without the need for lawyers or court proceedings).

As a practical matter, insurers rarely demand appraisal unless they are very confident in their evaluation of the amount of the loss. One of the reasons insurers will consider demanding appraisal in a case is when they believe the insured is considering suing for bad faith (*i.e.*, that the insured contends the insurer is low-balling the claim). If the outcome of the appraisal is at or very near the insurer's valuation of the amount of loss, then the appraisal demonstrates that the insurer's position was reasonable. It also then largely, if not completely, provides a defense if the insured nevertheless sues for bad faith. If the outcome is the opposite, that is, the appraisal award is significantly greater than the insurer's valuation of the loss, the insured's potential bad faith suit may have a greater likelihood of success, since the insured is then in the position of being able to argue that the insurer unreasonably undervalued the claim.

OTHER INSURANCE AND SERVICE AGREEMENTS

This policy condition addresses who should pay for a loss when it is covered by another insurance policy or by some other agreement such as a home warranty agreement or an extended warranty agreement.

When there is other insurance, the two insurers will share the loss in the proportion that their respective policy limits bear to each other. As a practical matter, if one insurer refuses to pay, the other insurer will often pay the entire claim, and then proceed to sue the first insurer to recover the unpaid share.

If there is a service agreement such as a home warranty plan, this condition provides that the insurance afforded by the policy will only pay the excess of any amounts payable under the service agreement.

SUITS AGAINST US

Suits against us (*no-action clauses*) address two separate concepts. First, this condition provides that no action can be brought against the insurer unless there has been full compliance by the insured with all the policy's terms and conditions. As a practical matter, the insurer cannot prevent the insured from filing a lawsuit. All this clause does is provide the insurer with a legal defense to a lawsuit by an insured when the insured fails to follow the policy requirements, such as refusing to submit to an examination under oath or failure to comply with the proof of loss requirements.

Second, this condition provides that suit must be brought within two years after the date of loss. This provision again cannot prevent an insured from filing a lawsuit against the insurer. It does, however, afford the insurer a legal defense to a lawsuit by the insured if that lawsuit is not filed within the two-year limit. Check your policy—many policies contain only a one-year period in which a suit must be brought. This provision is enforced in the same manner as is a statute of limitations.

In some states, the two-year period does not begin to run until the loss has become sufficiently apparent that a reasonable insured would know that his or her duty to give the insurer notice of the loss has been triggered. This is something that frequently becomes an issue in soils movement and foundation damage claims. Further, in some states, the *clock* on the two-year period stops running between the date when the insured gives notice of the claim and the date on which the insurer informs the insured of its coverage/claim decision.

Still further, if the insured is having difficulty completing the proof of loss, the insured and the insurer can enter into an agreement that the two-year limitation on suit period can be extended, just as they can agree that the time for submission of the proof of loss can be extended. Any such agreement necessarily should be confirmed in writing.

OUR OPTION

This condition permits the insurer to repair or replace any part of the damaged or destroyed property itself, instead of paying the insured.

LOSS PAYMENT

This condition addresses several issues, including to whom and when a claim payment will be made. This condition provides that payment will be made to the named insured unless some other person is named in the policy (*e.g.,* your spouse) or is legally entitled to receive payment (*e.g.,* your mortgage lender).

This condition further provides that loss payment will be made sixty days after the insurer's receipt of proof of loss and:

- ◆ the insured and the insurer agree to the amount of loss;
- ◆ there is an entry of a final judgment in the lawsuit; or,
- ◆ there is the filing of an appraisal award with the insurer.

ABANDONMENT OF PROPERTY

This condition provides that an insurer has no responsibility for property abandoned by an insured, whether for purposes of repair, demolition, disposal, or otherwise. In effect, this condition confirms that the insurer's duty in the event of a covered loss is fundamentally one of paying money.

MORTGAGE CLAUSE

This set of conditions sets forth the insurer's and mortgage lender's respective rights and obligations. (You can rest assured that most mortgage lenders are quite aware of their rights and obligations with respect to your policy.) The principal things that you need to know are that any loss payable for damage or destruction to the dwelling and other structures will be made both to you and your mortgage lender. Mortgage lenders often will require that claim payments be held in trust or in an account over which they have control in order to assure that the insured effects necessary repairs.

NO BENEFIT TO BAILEE

In effect, this provision is designed to assure that if a moving or storage company hired by you damages, loses, or destroys any of your property, it will be liable for that loss, not your homeowners insurer.

NUCLEAR HAZARD CLAUSE

This condition defines what constitutes *nuclear hazard* for purposes of the nuclear exclusion, and effectively provides that only direct loss by fire resulting from the nuclear hazard is covered. In the context of current times, this means that radioactive contamination of your property as the result of the leaks from a nuclear generating station would not be covered. Neither would radioactive contamination from a terrorist setting off a so-called dirty bomb.

RECOVERED PROPERTY

This condition details what will happen in the event stolen property is recovered that the insurer has paid for. It requires both parties to give notice to the other that property for which a claim has been made or paid has been recovered. This condition gives to the insured the choice of retaining the claim payment and surrendering the recovered property to the insurer or reclaiming the recovered property. If the insured elects to keep the recovered property, the loss payment will be adjusted down by the amount the insurer previously paid to the insured for loss of or damage to the property. This means that the insurer can deduct this amount from any outstanding amount of the claim from which payment will be made *or* that the insured will have to reimburse the insurer for the amount in question.

VOLCANIC ERUPTION

This condition provides that all volcanic eruptions that occur within a seventy-two-hour period will be considered one eruption. This provision is potentially relevant to how many:

- ◆ covered losses there may be and
- ◆ how many deductibles will apply.

POLICY PERIOD

This condition provides that the policy only applies to loss during the policy period. Under the law of many states, a property loss is deemed to have occurred during the policy period when the damage becomes apparent to the insured. Notwithstanding the fact that some kinds of losses occur gradually over multiple policy periods, this provision in effect provides that in such cases, only the policy in effect when the insured becomes aware (or should have become aware) of the loss will apply.

CONCEALMENT OR FRAUD

This is a highly important condition for all policyholders to be aware of. Concealment or fraud on the part of any person insured—at any time before or after a loss, including at the time of application—will void the policy of that insured altogether. There will be no refund of premiums.

Moreover, the consequences of misrepresentation, concealment, or fraud with respect to applying for an insurance policy or with respect to a claim are far-reaching. Most insurers maintain fraud databanks and share that information with each other and insurance regulatory authorities. If the fraud was in connection with a claim and you received a payment to which you were not entitled because of your fraud, you could also be subject to criminal prosecution. Committing a fraud on an insurance company has the potential of affecting your ability to obtain insurance in the future. If you cannot get insurance you may not be able to register your car in some states. Lacking insurance, you may not be able to operate certain kinds of businesses.

LOSS PAYABLE CLAUSE

This condition bears some parallels to the mortgage clause. It provides that if the declarations show a loss payee for specified items of personal property, the policy's definition of insured is amended to include the loss payee with respect to that property.

Chapter 9
Liability Coverages

The overall intent of the liability coverages of homeowners policies is to insure for liability to third parties arising out of the ownership, use, and occupancy of insured premises. The liability coverages of homeowners policies are not general liability coverages. Other liability exposures generally need to be insured separately. This can include the liability arising from business pursuits or from ownership and use of automobiles, watercraft, aircraft, and other vehicles (motorcycles, all terrain vehicles, snowmobiles, etc.).

The physical organization of the liability coverages of homeowners policies is essentially the same as that of the property coverages. The policy's *declarations* will specify the liability policy limits. If the policy's *definitions* appear at the beginning, rather than at the end of the policy, they follow the declarations and contain the definitions of terms pertinent to the liability coverages.

The *liability insuring agreement* (or coverage grant) generally appears in the policy as the next section following the *conditions* applicable to the property coverages. The *liability exclusions* follow next, followed in turn by the *liability additional coverages*. The *liability conditions* appear next. The basic homeowners policy concludes with the *conditions* that apply to both the property and the liability coverages. *Endorsements* that modify the property and liability coverages are attached at the end of the policy after the basic policy form ends.

INSURED CAPACITY ISSUES

As with the discussion of the property portion of the policies, the liability provisions will be examined based on the ISO HO 3 policy, and who is an insured and who is not marks the first step of analysis. Generally, resident relatives are insureds, as are resident nonrelatives under the age of 21 in the care of a named insured or a resident relative of the named insured. Unlike the case with property coverages of homeowners policies, there typically are no additional insured interests with respect to the liability coverages of homeowners policies. Correctly designating the named insureds under the liability coverages of homeowners policies where property that is the subject of the policy is owned by a trust is important. It is becoming increasingly common for persons to create trusts for estate planning and other purposes and to transfer titles to various kinds of property, including their personal residence, to the trust. If you have done this, you need to consult with your agent in order to assure that all persons are properly designated in the policy as insureds for purposes of the liability coverages. In most cases, *all* the following need to be designated as named insured:

- the trust itself;
- the trustees of the trust, designated by name and described as the trustees of the trust; and,
- (assuming the same individuals are the *de facto* owners and occupants of the premises) these individuals in their individual capacities.

INSURED LOCATIONS

The concept of *insured location* for purposes of the liability coverages of homeowners policies begins with the same definition as applicable to the property coverages (see p.43). Insured location includes the residence premises as that term is separately defined and then extends to various other locations.

The policy then limits that rather broad scope of insured location for purposes of the liability coverages by means of an exclusion that precludes coverage for liability arising out of premises:

◆ owned by an insured;

◆ rented to an insured; or,

◆ rented to others by an insured that is not an insured location.

Functionally, liability coverages are less location-specific than they are activity-specific. Thus, the geographic scope of coverage is controlled more by the nature of the liability-producing conduct than where the conduct takes place.

INSURING AGREEMENT

The liability coverage-insuring agreement of the homeowners policy establishes two basic duties on the insurer's part to the insured: the duty to defend and the duty to indemnify.

In contrast to the property coverages of the homeowners policy, the insuring agreement coverage grant of homeowners policies is relatively simple and can be summarized as follows. The insurer will pay damages that an insured becomes legally obligated (or liable) to pay because of *bodily injury* or *property damage* caused by an *occurrence*. The insurer will also defend the insured in suits seeking such damages by counsel chosen and paid for by the insurer.

The bodily injury or property damage must occur during the policy period. The insurer generally has the right to settle any claims or suit against the insured at its discretion. The insurer's duty to defend terminates upon payment of the full liability policy limits.

Thus, the meanings of *bodily injury*, *property damage*, and *occurrence* are crucial to an understanding of how liability coverages work. Occurrence is the most central concept applicable to liability insurance. The definition of occurrence in the ISO HO 3 homeowners policy states:

> *Occurrence means an accident, including continuous or repeated exposure to substantially the same general harmful conditions, which result during the policy period in: (a) bodily injury; or, (b) property damage.*

The concept of coverage for liability arising from accidents is how the fortuity element essential to insurance is incorporated into liability coverages. An *accident* is an unintentional, unexpected, chance occurrence or event. The *occurrence* is the causal event and the bodily injury or property damage is the result or consequence of the occurrence.

It is the liability-producing act or conduct that must be an accident, not the resulting bodily injury or property damage. Bodily injury or property damage that is unintended or unexpected by an insured is not covered if it is the product of intentional, nonaccidental conduct. Coverage turns on the insured's intent to commit the act in question, not on his or her state of mind in performing the act. Therefore, it does not matter whether the insured expected or intended his or her conduct to cause harm. An accident can result from a deliberate act, but only when some additional, unexpected, independent, and unforeseen event happens that causes the injury or damage in question.

PERSONAL INJURY

This is a good time to discuss the personal injury coverage that is included in some homeowners policies, or that is an optional coverage to be added by an endorsement to others (such as the ISO HO 3 policy). As noted, while there are some variations from insurer to insurer, personal injury liability coverage extends to five basic categories of acts or conduct. These include:

1. false arrest, detention, or imprisonment;
2. libel, slander, defamation, or product disparagement;
3. malicious prosecution (which may include abuse of process);
4. wrongful eviction, wrongful entry, or violation of right of private occupancy; and,
5. invasion of or violation of right of privacy.

None of these categories of conduct can be an accident. As a result, most homeowners liability coverages refer to the covered events as *offenses*, rather than attempting to subject them to the policy's occurrence/accident requirement. There is a temporal difference between the accident-based bodily injury and property damage coverage and the offense-based personal injury coverage. Coverage applies to bodily injury and property damage that occurs during the policy period, regardless of when the occurrence that causes the bodily injury or property damage takes place.

In contrast, the offense-based personal injury coverage applies to offenses that the injured commits during the policy period. As noted, the personal injury offenses involve intentional conduct. There are, however, limitations on the scope of coverage for these categories of intentional acts. (These are discussed in the context of exclusions that apply to the personal injury coverages.)

Personal Injury Additional Coverages

There is a single additional coverage under the ISO personal injury endorsement—for loss assessments up to $1,000 each assessment for the insured's share of loss assessments made as the result of covered personal injury. This provision is substantially similar to the bodily injury and property and additional damage for loss assessments.

BODILY INJURY

Bodily injury means bodily harm, sickness, or disease, including required care, loss of services, and death that results. There really are not any hidden concepts here. Everyone can readily appreciate that if someone is hurt as the result of an accident for which you may be held liable, that person's damages include many things, such as:

- his or her medical and hospital bills;
- past and future wage loss or earning capacity;
- costs of ongoing care; and,
- damages for his or her inability to enjoy the activities enjoyed prior to the injury.

What can be an issue is whether mental or emotional distress constitutes bodily injury in the absence of physical injury. A growing trend in the law is the view that emotional distress that is the product of noncovered conduct does not constitute bodily injury within the meaning of standard liability policy definitions of bodily injury. For example, emotional distress that is the product of economic loss, such as the loss in value of an investment or savings, does not constitute bodily injury under this view.

PROPERTY DAMAGE

The standard ISO HO 3 homeowners policy contains the following definition of property damage.

> *Property damage means physical injury to, destruction of, or loss of use of tangible property.*

The concept of *physical injury* to tangible property is central to an understanding of the property damage coverage of liability policies. This physical injury to tangible property requirement has the effect of excluding coverage for damages claims based on injury to nontangible property interests. Even the *loss of use* portion of the property damage definition is tied to *tangible property.*

Tangible property means property having physical substance, apparent to the senses. Examples of intangible property are things such as easements, leasehold interests, licenses, patents, copyrights, lost profits, loss of goodwill, loss of the expected benefit of a bargain, and loss of value of an investment. Diminution in value of an investment constitutes economic loss, not property damage. However, diminution in value of tangible property as the result of physical injury can be used as a measure of damages resulting from physical injury to tangible property.

EXAMPLE: Let's say an adjoining landowner has an easement across your property for access to the street or highway. You build a fence across your property, including across the easement, that prevents access.

The adjoining landowner sues you. His lawsuit would not constitute a covered property damage claim. Your interference with his easement is interference with intangible property rights. The physical injury element is also missing.

Another example of a noncovered economic loss claim would be a suit against you arising out of your sale to another person of a car or motorcycle that breaks down and requires expensive repairs shortly after the sale. There is no property damage here. Rather, the essence of the claim is an economic loss—loss of the buyer's expected benefit of the bargain. The buyer paid a certain amount for the car or motorcycle on the expectation that it was in good working order, when, had its true condition been known, the fair purchase price would have been much less.

Similar comments would apply to a suit against you by a buyer of a house for alleged nondisclosure or concealment of defects in or damage to the house, such as nonpermitted alterations or remodeling.

What about loss of use property damage claims? An example of a covered loss of use claim is as follows. Your residence is situated upslope from one of your neighbors. The hillside, on your property, becomes unstable, causing the local authorities to order your neighbor and his family out of their home until the hillside can be stabilized. Your neighbor has lost use of tangible property, his house and premises, during the period required to stabilize the hillside. He would have a loss of use property damage claim against you. Some homeowners policies' property damage definitions only extend loss of use coverage to tangible property that has been physically injured. Thus, assuming the same facts as the preceeding example, under a policy whose property damage definition only extends to loss of use of tangible property that has been physically injured, your neighbor's suit against you would not constitute a covered property damage lawsuit.

DUTY TO DEFEND AND RELATED ISSUES

As noted, the liability coverage of a homeowners policy includes two primary promises by the insurer—the duty to defend (to provide you with a legal defense to lawsuits seeking covered damages) and the duty to indemnify (to pay covered judgments or settlements on your behalf). These two related duties are governed by different standards in a number of respects.

The existence of the duty to defend is determined at the outset of the lawsuit against you and depends on whether there is a potential for an award of damages against you that would be covered by the policy. Under the ISO HO 3 homeowners policy, the insurer is expressly obligated to provide you with a defense to lawsuits that are groundless, false, or fraudulent, as well as lawsuits that have some actual or potential merit.

In some jurisdictions, whether a duty to defend a suit exists is determined solely by comparing the allegations of the complaint in the lawsuit against you with the terms of the policy. This is done without regard to any facts known at the time of the lawsuit that are extrinsic to (that is, not alleged or stated in) the complaint. This approach can cut both ways. In some cases, the insured may be aware of and communicate facts to his or her insurer that are extrinsic to the complaint and that suggest that coverage exists. However, the insurer need not consider them and can deny a duty to defend if the allegations of the complaint do not bring the lawsuit within coverage. On the other hand, there may be a situation in which the complaint alleges facts that trigger a duty to defend and the insurer knows of facts extrinsic to the complaint that would otherwise negate a duty to defend. In this case, the insurer cannot consider those facts and must provide a defense solely on the basis of the complaint's allegations.

In a growing number of jurisdictions, facts extrinsic to the third-party claimant's complaint that are known at the outset of the lawsuit can be considered by the insurer in determining whether a defense is owed.

The costs of defense are covered in addition to the policy limit, meaning that the insurer pays for the fees and costs incurred by the lawyer who defends you in the lawsuit as well as a resulting judgment or settlement. These costs can include filing fees for motions, photocopying charges, costs of obtaining evidence with which to defend the lawsuit, court reporter and deposition costs, etc.

Because legal fees and costs can be prohibitively high for most persons, the law in most states requires that the duty to defend be construed broadly and that the insurer makes its coverage decision promptly. Generally, any doubt as to whether a duty to defend exists is resolved in the insured's favor.

Sometimes the facts alleged in the third-party claimants complaint suggest the possibility of liability on the insured's part both for damages that would be covered and damages that would not be covered. Under most states' laws, the insurer is obligated to defend the entire lawsuit, not just the claims that are potentially covered. A common example is a bodily injury suit based on a physical altercation in which the claimant alleges that the defendant's conduct was either accidental or intentional. Another common example is a libel or slander suit that suggest that the defendant uttered the libel or slander with knowledge of the falsity of his or her statements.

In such cases, the insurer will generally defend a subject to a *reservation of rights*. In a reservation of rights letter, the insurer informs the insured that it will be providing a defense, and points out the factual and legal grounds as to why coverage may not exist. It then reserves the right to refuse to pay a judgment or settlement if the facts adjudicated in the lawsuit establish one or more grounds under the policy for denying coverage. Sometimes, insurers also reserve the right to withdraw from the defense of a lawsuit if facts become known before the lawsuit is concluded that establish that no coverage exists.

In many states, when an insurer issues a reservation of rights that creates a conflict of interest between the insured and the insurer, the insured may be entitled to be defended, at the insurer's expense, by counsel of the insured's own choosing, rather than by counsel hired by the insurer. The insurer may also be required to relinquish control over the defense and settlement of the suit to the insured and the insured's selected counsel.

If you find yourself in a situation in which your insurer has issued a reservation of rights with respect to a lawsuit against you, consult an attorney. You must find one at your own expense to advise you whether, under your state's local law, you are entitled to a defense by counsel of your own choosing. Next, you must determine whether you should exercise that right.

Some homeowners policies' liability insuring agreements state that the insurer has no obligation to pay for a defense by counsel selected by the insured due to a coverage dispute between the insurer and the insured. Such provisions are likely to be held unenforceable. What may be permissible is for the insurer to include a provision that permits the insured to select his or her defense counsel from a list of law firms supplied by the insurer in the event the insurer issues a qualifying reservation of rights.

While an insurer has the right to investigate and settle claims, it only has an obligation to defend *suits*—that is, formal court proceedings. As a practical matter, many, if not most, insurers will hire defense counsel if a claim is made that shows serious potential to evolve into a suit.

Second, a duty to defend arises upon notice by the insurer to the insurer of the suit. Such notice is also referred to as *tender* of the defense of the lawsuit to the insurer.

Termination of the duty to defend can be a more complex issue. First, the policy expressly provides that the duty to defend ends when the insurer has paid the full liability policy limits and settlement of the suit or in satisfaction of the judgment entered in the lawsuit. Full payment of the policy limit is also termed *exhaustion* of the limits of the policy.

The duty to defend also terminates if the suit is concluded and no damages are awarded against the insured, unless the claimant takes an appeal. In this case, the duty to defend continues and requires the insurer to defend on appeal too.

Finally, insurers sometimes unilaterally withdraw a defense upon learning facts that, in their view, negate coverage. This is a permissible action under the law of most jurisdictions. If the insurer is mistaken, however, the consequences of an erroneous unilateral withdrawal of a defense can be substantially the same as those consequences of an erroneous denial of a defense at the outset of the lawsuit against the insured. For this reason, insurers often will withdraw a defense only after a court has ruled that no coverage exists in a declaratory relief action. When there is a coverage dispute between the insured and the insurer, either may institute a declaratory judgment lawsuit in order to have the coverage issues decided by a judge.

DUTY TO INDEMNIFY

The existence of a duty to indemnify is determined at the end of the third-party claimant's lawsuit against the insured based on the facts as adjudicated in that lawsuit. If the insurer has made a decision to settle the case and not let it go to trial, its payment of the settlement is covered under the policy's indemnity coverage. Virtually all settlements include denials of liability, even if one of the reasons for the insurer's decision to settle may have been that the case was one of probable liability. Insurers settle cases brought against insureds for a lot of reasons, including a weighing of whether the costs of defense and the risks of an adverse justify proceeding with trial. Insurers have to be cool-headed and practical. The more money they can save through judicious settlements, the lower their costs of doing business are and, ultimately, the lower the costs of insurance for all their policyholders will be.

Unlike the *potential for coverage* standard for deciding whether a duty to defend exists, a duty to indemnify is determined by an *actual coverage* standard. Often, this is clear—when the jury rules for the plaintiff in the lawsuit against the insured, it is implicit from the jury's decision that they have decided that the facts determine the coverage issues and thus the insurer's obligation to pay.

Sometimes, however, the facts as adjudicated in the action against the insured leave the coverage issues unclear. Any number of things can happen. The insurer can simply agree to pay the judgment to conclude the lawsuit. Or, the insurer will sometimes pay the judgment subject to a reservation of rights to litigate the coverage issues in a separate lawsuit called a *declaratory relief action*. A declaratory relief action is a lawsuit by an insured or an insurer in which the court is asked to review the facts and the policy and to decide whether the claim is or is not covered.

When a homeowners policy provides personal injury coverage, the same issues relating to the existence of a duty to defend and duty to indemnify exist as is with the bodily injury and property damage coverage. The only real difference is the nature of the insured's conduct and resulting injury for which the claimant is suing the insured for damages.

MEDICAL PAYMENTS COVERAGE

Medical payments coverage is essentially a low-limit, no-fault coverage intended to deal with low-value bodily injury claims on a quick and informal basis. Typical medical payments limits of liability range between $1,000 and $10,000 per person, per accident. The medical payments coverage of homeowners policies is generally included as part of the basic policy premium without any separate or additional premium.

The insuring agreement of the medical payments coverage of the ISO HO 3 homeowners policy provides that the insurer will pay necessary medical expenses that are incurred or are medically ascertained within three years from the date of an accident that causes bodily injury. Medical expenses are defined as reasonable charges for medical, surgical, X-ray, dental, ambulance, hospital, professional nursing, prosthetic devices, and funeral expenses. The medical payments coverage does not apply to persons insured under the policy.

For medical payments coverage to apply, the person seeking payment must have been on an insured location with the permission of an insured. The medical payments coverage also applies to a person off an insured location if the bodily injury in question:

- arises out of conditions on the insured location or on the ways immediately adjoining (*i.e.,* streets, roads, sidewalks, etc.,); *and,*
- is caused by the activities of an insured; *or*
- is caused by a residence employee (housekeeper, gardener, nanny, etc.) in the course of the residence employee's employment by an insured; *or,*
- is caused by an animal owned or in the care of an insured.

Medical payments coverage usually does not vary greatly from one insurer to another due to the relatively low exposure to loss that such provisions present to insurers. Nonetheless, the medical payments coverages present a valuable resource in the event of a minor injury occurring to someone on your premises that comes within the scope of that coverage. Often, in such cases, prompt payment by your insurer under the medical payments coverages may help to avoid a later lawsuit. The prompt attention to the situation and prompt payment of the injured party's medical bills can take some of the sting out of an accident, leaving the injured parties less disposed to sue.

The medical payments coverage is limited by exclusions and will be reviewed in the discussion of all the exclusions that apply to a homeowner's liability coverages in Chapter 10.

ADDITIONAL COVERAGES

Liability coverages also have some additional coverages. Some of these additional coverages can be significant in their impact.

Claims Expenses

The first category listed under additional coverages is *claims expenses.* These are items that relate primarily to the defense of lawsuits. There are four subcategories of claims expenses that are covered.

First, they include expenses the insurer incurs (this includes the fees and expenses of defense counsel plus costs taxed against the insured such as:

- filing fees;
- jury fees;
- deposition costs;
- costs of service of process;
- witness fees;
- transcripts of court proceedings;
- photocopying costs; and,
- attorneys' fees.

Second, the liability additional coverages include coverage for premiums for bonds required in suits that the insured appeals. The most likely application of this provision is if there is an adverse judgment against the insured and a decision is made to appeal the judgment. Universally, in order to prevent the winning party from collecting on his or her judgment while the case is on appeal, the losing party must post an appeal bond. If an appeal bond is posted, the winning party cannot engage in collection efforts until the appeal has been decided.

Appeal bonds are not cheap. An appeal bond usually must be posted in an amount ranging from 150% to 200% of the amount of the judgment. This is to cover the judgment as well as the interest accruing on the judgment while the appeal remains pending. Further, an insurer is required only to pay for the premium for an appeal bond, not to provide the collateral for the 150% to 200% bond amount. If the amount of the judgment against the insured exceeds the liability policy limit, the insurer is only required to pay that portion of the premium for the appeal bond that is in proportion to the amount of the judgment within policy limits.

As a practical matter, the fact that an insurer has no obligation to collateralize an appeal bond is a reason why many adverse judgments against insureds are paid, no appeal is taken, and the case ends. A great many insureds are simply unable, or unwilling, to post collateral for an appeal bond, particularly when there is a substantial risk that the insured could become liable on the bond and forfeit the collateral.

Third, claim expenses coverage includes reasonable expenses incurred by an insured at the insurer's request. This includes actual loss of earnings, up to $250 per day, for assisting the insurer (and hired defense counsel) in the investigation or defense of a suit.

Fourth, the liability additional coverages include postjudgment interest that accrues prior to the time the insurer either pays the judgment or pays a court that portion of the judgment for which the insurer does not contest coverage.

First Aid Expenses

The next category of liability additional coverages is for first aid expenses incurred by an insured for covered bodily injury. This coverage excludes first aid expenses for bodily injury to an insured, and is in addition to both the personal liability limit as well as the separate limit applicable to the medical payments coverage. *First aid* is not defined in the policy and should be interpreted according to its ordinary meaning.

Damage to Property of Others

This additional coverage extends coverage on a replacement cost basis, up to $1,000 per occurrence for property damage to property of others caused by an insured. There are some exclusions to this coverage. This additional coverage does not apply to any loss to the extent it is payable under the first-party property coverages of the policy, nor to loss to property owned by an insured. Property damage that is caused intentionally by an insured over the age of thirteen is also not covered. This additional coverage also excludes coverage for property damage to property owned by or rented to a tenant of an insured or resident of the named insured's household.

The damage to property of others coverage does not apply to loss arising out of an insured's business, out of premises owned, granted, or controlled by an insured other than the insured location, or out of the ownership, maintenance, occupancy, operation, use, loading or unloading of aircraft, watercraft, hovercraft, or motor vehicles.

Loss Assessment

The loss assessment additional coverage provides for up to $1,000 for the named insured's share of a loss assessment charged against the named insured as owner or tenant of the residence premises by a condominium, homeowners, or cooperative association. This covers situations when the assessment is the result of covered bodily injury, property damage, or liability for a director, officer, or trustee while acting in that capacity. The person must have been elected by the association's members and services without pay.

This additional coverage has some qualifications and limitations. The policy period condition does not apply—loss assessments imposed on members by homeowners associations virtually always occur long after the event that ultimately gives rise to the assessment takes place. The policy makes clear that the $1,000 limit applies to all loss arising out of any one accident or covered act of a board member, regardless of the number of assessments imposed.

EXAMPLE: If a board were to impose a $100 a month assessment arising out of one accident for a period of 15 months, the maximum amount recoverable by the insured would be $1,000. If the board were to impose a $100 per month assessment for a period of five months, and then six months later, impose a $100 per month assessment for a period of ten months arising out of a second and separate accident, the amount recoverable would be $1,500.

This additional coverage expressly excludes coverage for assessments charged against the named insured or the homeowners association by any governmental body. Thus, if your city imposes an improvement assessment for street repaving or some other project, no coverage exists under this provision.

Chapter 10
Liability Coverage Exclusions

Like the property coverages, the grant of coverage of personal liability in home-owners policies is limited by exclusions. Some of the exclusions address relatively specific and narrow subject areas. Others address broader subject areas so as to reinforce the distinctions between personal liability out of the owner-ship, maintenance, or occupancy of insured premises and liabilities arising out of business pursuits or activities, workers compensation, motor vehicles, or pro-fessional services, which should be insured under separate policies.

These exclusions are discussed in the order in which they appear in the standard ISO HO 2 and HO 3 homeowners policies.

MOTOR VEHICLE LIABILITY EXCLUSION

This exclusion precludes coverage under both the liability and medical pay-ments coverages for *motor vehicle liability*, if at the time of occurrence, the involved motor vehicle was either registered for use on public streets or was required to have been registered. In addition, this exclusion precludes cov-erage if, at the time of occurrence, the motor vehicle was being used in any prearranged, organized race, speed contest, or other competition.

The *motor vehicle liability* exclusion also precludes coverage for occurrences arising out of motor vehicles that are: rented to others; used to carry persons or cargo for charge; or used for any business purposes, except for motorized golf carts while on a golfing facility.

There are some exceptions to this exclusion. Where none of these excluded categories applies, the motor vehicle liability exclusion does not apply if the motor vehicle out of which the claim arises is:

- in dead storage on an insured location;
- used solely to service an insured's residence;
- designed to assist the handicapped and at the time of an occurrence is:
  - being used to assist a handicapped person or
  - is parked on an insured location;
- designed for recreational use off public roads and is:
  - not owned by an insured or
  - owned by an insured, provided the occurrence takes place on an insured location; or,
- a motorized golf cart as defined by policy language.

These provisions are intended to highlight the distinctions between those forms of motor vehicle liability that should be the subject of an auto liability policy and those that fall within the scope of personal liability that is the subject of coverage of a homeowners policy.

EXPECTED OR INTENDED INJURY

This exclusion precludes liability for medical payments for bodily injury or property damage that is expected or intended by an insured. This is regardless of whether the bodily injury or property damage is of a different kind, quality, or degree than initially expected or is sustained by a different person, entity, or property than initially expected or intended.

There are important points that you need to understand about the expected or intended exclusion. First, expected or intended losses are not insurable because they are not fortuitous. Many states have statutory willful acts exclusions that are implied by law into all policies. In many other states, there are not statutory willful acts exclusions per se, but the same result is implied as a matter of public policy. In some states, however, the exclusion must be expressly included.

Second, coverage is excluded for bodily injury or property damage that is expected or intended by *an insured*. In a majority of states, the use of *an* or *any* rather than *the* insured is likely to have the result that no coverage will exist for a so-called innocent co-insured. This covers situations in which an injured party attempts to impose vicarious liability on one insured for the intentional acts of another insured.

Third, excuses—for example, that you did not mean to hit someone as hard as you actually did—are not going to render this exclusion inapplicable.

The expected or intended exclusion has an exception for bodily injury resulting from the use of reasonable force by an insured to protect persons or property. In this context, reasonable force to protect persons or property should be considered only that necessary for self-defense (or the defense of others) or to prevent a property crime, such as burglary, theft, or arson. In most states, a person may only use lethal force to protect him- or herself or another, when that person is *objectively* threatened by lethal force on the part of an assailant.

In many if not most states, the use of lethal force is never permissible to prevent a property crime, except when the commission of a property crime threatens the lives of others (for example, arson, in certain limited circumstances).

The amount of force that may be permissibly employed to protect persons or property is the minimum level necessary to meet the threat presented, judged on an objective, not a subjective, standard. If your use of force in response to a threat to yourself, to another person, or to property exceeds the permissible level, you will be deemed the aggressor. This gives rights on the part of the other person to use reasonable force to deter what is now, from a legal standpoint, your assault on him or her.

The lessons you need to take home from these admonitions are as follows.

- Keep your cool.
- Do not escalate confrontations.
- Do not enlist the assistance of a bunch of buddies to take matters into your own hands.
- If you go over the line, or even if it is a close call, you may jeopardize your right to insurance coverage, and should at minimum expect a defense subject to the insurer's reservation of right to deny paying a resulting judgment against you.
- If you are subject to criminal prosecution, your insurer has *absolutely no* obligation to provide you with a defense counsel in your criminal case.
- A conviction in a criminal case can serve as a basis for denying coverage completely in a civil lawsuit arising from the same incident.

BUSINESS EXCLUSION

The *business*—or to use former terminology, *business pursuits*—exclusion, is one of the most important and long-standing exclusions to the liability coverages of homeowners policies. Until the recent past, the verbiage of the business definition was very simple and straightforward. If the activity in question had *any* business or profit motive, then no coverage existed.

Things have changed. The lines between business activities and personal activities have become more complicated. As a result, the definition of business is more complex, as is the business exclusion.

The definition of business now reads a *trade, profession, or occupation engaged in on full-time, part-time, or occasional basis and any other activity engaged in for money or other compensation except the following:…*

There are four categories of exceptions. First, there are activities not falling within the following three categories, for which no insured receives more than $2,000 in total compensation for the 12-month period prior to the beginning of the policy.

Second, volunteer activities for which no money is received other than reimbursement of expenses incurred to perform the activity are not deemed to be a business.

Third, providing home day care services for which the insured receives no compensation other than mutual exchange of such services from others is not deemed a business.

Fourth, the definition of business does not include providing home day care services to a relative of an insured.

The business exclusion itself provides that the liability and medical payments coverages do not apply to bodily injury or property damage arising out of or in connection with a business conducted from an insured location or engaged in by an insured. It does not matter whether or not the business is owned or operated by an insured or employs an insured. The business exclusion further states that it includes but is not limited to acts or omissions involving services or duties rendered and promises owed or implied to be provided because of the nature of the business.

The use of the phrases *arising out of*, or *in connection with*, in the business exclusion renders it a very broad exclusion. These phrases require only a minimal, incidental relationship between bodily injury and an insured's business activities to render the exclusion applicable.

There are some exceptions to the business exclusion. The most common would involve renting part of the residence premises or using portions of it as an office, school, studio, or private garage.

Finally, the business exclusion does not apply to an insured who is under the age of 21 and involved in a part-time or occasional, self-employed business without any employees. For example, your daughter's baby-sitting for pay or your son's mowing lawns, raking leaves, or shoveling snow for pay would not fall into the business exclusion.

PROFESSIONAL SERVICES

The professional services exclusion is a close companion to the business exclusion and precludes coverage for bodily injury or property damage arising out of the rendering of or failure to render professional services. The various states differ in their interpretation of professional services. Some states interpret the phrase as meaning traditional, learned professions, such as medicine, law, accounting, and engineering. Other states interpret professional services far more broadly—including any activity conducted for compensation that requires any specialized skill or knowledge that is not possessed by the average person—and is not limited to traditional learned professions.

Professional services exclusions also are standard exclusions in commercial liability policies. If you engage in or provide services for remuneration, you may have a professional services exposure that needs to be separately insured under an errors and omissions policy particular to the type of services you are rendering.

INSURED'S PREMISES NOT AN INSURED LOCATION

This exclusion expressly provides that the liability and medical payments coverages do not apply to bodily injury or property damage arising at premises that do not qualify as insured locations.

WAR

This exclusion precludes coverage for bodily injury and property damage caused directly or indirectly by war, which is defined in a manner that probably would be ruled not to include acts of terrorism, whether domestic or foreign.

COMMUNICABLE DISEASE

The communicable disease exclusion precludes coverage for bodily injury and property damage arising out of the transmission of a communicable disease by an insured. Insurers first sought to have exclusions in their homeowners policies for sexually-transmitted diseases in the late 1970s and early 1980s. During that time, herpes type II (*i.e.,* genital herpes) cases first became widespread and insurers found themselves defending a great many lawsuits arising out of such claims.

After AIDS and HIV became an issue of public concern, it was claimed by gay-rights and certain ethnic-group rights organizations that exclusions for sexually-transmitted diseases were discriminatory. As a result, the exclusion was broadened by substitution of the phrase communicable disease for sexually-transmitted disease.

SEXUAL MOLESTATION, CORPORAL PUNISHMENT, OR ABUSE

This exclusion precludes liability and medical payments coverage for bodily injury or property damage arising out of sexual molestation, corporal punishment, or physical or mental abuse. Insurers have included some form of sexual molestation exclusion in the liability portions of homeowners policies for some time now. These exclusions have generated a great deal of litigation over a variety of issues. The insurance industry continues through its drafting efforts to attempt to make clear that coverage should not be capable of being purchased for claims of this nature.

CONTROLLED SUBSTANCES

The controlled substances exclusion precludes liability and medical payment coverage for bodily injury and property damage arising out of the use, sale, manufacture, delivery, transfer, or possession of controlled substances. There is an exception for bodily injury or property damage arising out of the legitimate use of prescription drugs by a person following a licensed physician's orders.

Examples of how this exclusion might apply include the following.

- If an insured injures another person or damages another's property while under the influence of a controlled substance, the bodily injury or property damage would arise from the use of a controlled substance and coverage would most likely be precluded.

- If a fire or explosion resulted from an insured's illegal drug lab and damaged adjoining properties, coverage would be precluded for any resulting lawsuits against the insured.

- If an insured furnished controlled substances to a third party, who injured him- or herself while under the influence of the controlled substance, coverage would be precluded for a resulting bodily injury suit against the insured.

CONTRACTUAL LIABILITY

This exclusion applies only to the liability coverage. It does not apply to the medical payments coverages. The contractual liability exclusion has two parts. First, coverage is precluded for loss assessments by homeowners associations except as is provided for in the liability additional coverages, as outlined in Chapter 9.

Second, this exclusion precludes coverage for liability of an insured under any contract or agreement. There are two exceptions to this latter portion of the contractual liability exclusion. The exclusion does not apply to written contracts that directly relate to the ownership, maintenance, or use of the insured locations. Nor does this exclusion apply to written contracts under which the insured assumes the liability of others, prior to any occurrence, except as would otherwise be excluded by other policy provisions.

OWNED PROPERTY

This exclusion also applies only to the liability coverage. It precludes coverage for property owned by an insured and applies to costs and expenses incurred by an insured or others to repair, replace, enhance, restore, or maintain such property to prevent bodily injury or property damage to others, whether on or off premises. The purpose of this exclusion is to limit the coverage applicable to an insured's own property to that which is afforded by the first-party property coverages of a homeowners policy.

RENTAL PROPERTY

The rental property exclusion applies only to the liability coverage and precludes coverage for property damage to property rented to, occupied by, used by, or in the care of an insured. There is an exception to this exclusion for property damage caused by fire, smoke, or explosion.

WORKERS COMPENSATION

The workers compensation exclusion applies only to the liability coverage and precludes coverage for bodily injury to any person who is eligible to receive benefits provided or required to be provided by any insured under any:

   ◆ workers compensation law;
   ◆ nonoccupational disability law; or,
   ◆ occupational disease law.

In many states now, homeowners policies are required to include workers compensation coverage for residence employees. Under the ISO HO 2 and HO 3 policies, it is added by way of an endorsement to the policy. Many insurers include workers compensation coverage for residence employees (housekeepers, gardeners, nannies, etc.—whether resident or not) within their basic policy forms, usually as one of the liability additional coverages.

NUCLEAR

This exclusion is straightforward and precludes coverage for bodily injury or property damage for which an insured under the policy is also an insured under a nuclear energy liability policy issued by various entities. Nuclear exclusions are standard exclusions under policies issued to almost every personal lines and homeowners insured. In a practical sense, when the provisions of the nuclear exclusion are reviewed, there are few conceivable ways in which a homeowner could have such a loss exposure.

BODILY INJURY TO INSUREDS

This exclusion precludes coverage for bodily injury to yourself or to another person qualifying as an insured under the first two paragraphs of a HO 2 or HO 3 policy's definition of an insured. This exclusion also extends to any claim or suit against an insured to repay or share damages with another person who may be obligated to pay damages because of bodily injury to an insured.

In other words, this latter provision excludes coverage for a suit by a third party against an insured for indemnity or for contribution to sums that the third party has or may be held liable to pay as damages for bodily injury to another person qualifying as an insured. The following example should help you to understand what this means.

EXAMPLE: A third party is present at a party at your house. He engages in an altercation with one of your sons and injures him. Your son sues the third party and recovers damages for his injuries. The third party turns around and sues you for indemnity or contribution. He does this on the ground that some act or omission on your part was the cause of the injuries to your son—for example, providing alcohol. Therefore he claims that you should be held liable for some or all of the damages. This provision would exclude coverage for such a suit.

MEDICAL PAYMENTS COVERAGES EXCLUSIONS

The next group of exclusions is a short group that applies only to the medical payments coverages, several of which are substantially similar to many of the previous group of exclusions that apply only to the liability coverages.

Residence Employees Off Premises

This exclusion precludes medical payments coverage for residence employees if bodily injury occurs away from an insured premises *and* does not arise out of or occur within the course of employment of the residence employee by an insured. Both of these conditions must exist for this exclusion to apply. As a result, this is a narrow exclusion. In other words, if bodily injury to a residence employee occurs off premises, but within the course of employment, the medical payments coverage applies. Similarly, if the bodily injury to a residence employee occurs at an insured location, the medical payments coverage applies even if the bodily injury did not occur within the course of employment.

Workers Compensation

As with the liability coverage, the medical payments coverage does not apply to bodily injury to any person eligible to receive benefits pursuant to any workers compensation, nonoccupational disability, or occupational disease law. As with the liability coverage, workers compensation coverage is required to be provided by homeowners policies in many states.

Nuclear

As with all other portions of the ISO HO 2 and HO 3 homeowners policies, medical payments coverage does not apply to bodily injury from nuclear reaction, radiation, or radioactive contamination, however caused.

Residents

This exclusion provides that the medical payments coverage does not apply to any person who regularly resides on any part of any insured location, except for residence employees.

Other Comments

Exclusions applicable to the liability and medical payments coverages do not vary widely from insurer to insurer. Some insurers include exclusions for punitive or exemplary damages. In most, but not all, states, the punitive damages are noninsurable as a matter of law, although there are a few states where there is no such public policy. In those states, if insurers wish to avoid coverage for punitive damages, a separate exclusion needs to be included.

PERSONAL INJURY LIABILITY COVERAGE EXCLUSIONS

As noted, many homeowners policies also include personal injury liability coverage. Under the ISO HO 3 policy, if an insured wishes to add personal injury coverage, it is added by an endorsement. In policies that include personal injury coverage within the basic policy form, the personal injury exclusions are intermingled with the bodily injury and property damage exclusions.

The ISO personal injury endorsement's insuring agreement contains the same duties to defend and indemnify as does the bodily injury and property damage insuring agreement. Some of the personal injury exclusions are substantially similar to several of the bodily injury and property damage exclusions. The personal injury exclusions are as follows, in the order in which they appear.

Intentional Acts

This exclusion precludes coverage for personal injury caused by or at the direction of an insured with knowledge the act would violate the rights of another and would inflict personal injury.

Knowledge of Falsity

This exclusion precludes coverage for *personal injury* arising out of oral or written publication of material, if done by or at the direction of an insured, with knowledge of its falsity. This is a specific example in the context of coverage for libel, slander, product disparagement, or invasion of privacy of conduct that also would be precluded under the expected or intended exclusion applicable to the bodily injury or property damage coverages.

Prior Publication

This exclusion precludes coverage for personal injury arising out of the oral or written publication of material whose first publication takes place before the policy. The prior publication exclusion is another one that applies to the defamation offenses and privacy violation offenses. It recognizes that the same defamatory material or material that invades a person's right of privacy may be published several times. It provides, consistent with the personal injury insuring agreement, that coverage applies only to offenses that are first committed while the policy is in effect.

The law that determines whether a publication during the policy period, which contains material published prior to the policy period but varies in some way from the previous publication, is a sufficient basis to trigger the coverage and avoid the application of the first publication exclusion, varies state by state. This is a highly factually dependent inquiry in which the outcome will vary from case to case.

Criminal Acts

This exclusion precludes coverage for personal injury arising out of criminal acts committed by or at the direction of an insured. In the context of the applicable personal injury coverage offenses, this exclusion is more likely to be applicable to the false imprisonment, wrongful entry, or eviction categories of personal injury offenses than it is to the defamation categories of personal injury offenses.

Contractual Liability

This exclusion is largely the same as the second part of the bodily injury and property damage contractual liability exclusion.

Employment Related

This exclusion precludes coverage for personal injury sustained by a person as the result of an offense directly or indirectly related to the employment of that person by an insured. This is an example in which there is an attempt to keep the boundaries of personal liability and business liability clear and separate.

Business Activities

This exclusion is substantially identical to the bodily injury and property damage business exclusion and needs no further explanation.

Compensated Civic or Public Activities

This exclusion precludes coverage for personal injury arising out of public or civic activities by an insured for which the insured receives pay. This is a liability exposure that should be covered by the insurer of the governmental or other body for which an insured performs civic or public activities, such as a homeowners association.

Personal Injury to Insureds

This exclusion is essentially identical to the bodily injury to insureds exclusion of the bodily injury and property damage coverages.

Pollution

This exclusion precludes personal injury coverage arising out of the actual, alleged, or threatened discharge of pollutants. It contains an insurance industry standard definition of pollutants. This exclusion is included in the personal injury endorsement because common theories of liability asserted in pollution lawsuits by adjoining or nearby landowners or by governmental bodies include nuisance and trespass. These claims can at times fall into the *wrongful entry group* of personal injury offenses, depending on how those defenses are defined.

Pollution Remediation Expense

This precludes personal injury coverage for the costs arising out of requests, demands, or orders that an insured test for, monitor, clean up, remove, contain, treat, detoxify, neutralize, or in any way respond to or assess the effects of the pollutants.

The best way to distinguish between the prior exclusion and this exclusion is that the prior exclusion is aimed at damages claims, whereas this exclusion is aimed at the costs and expenses of complying with federal and state pollution remediation statutes. The latter costs and expenses are sometimes characterized as not constituting damages. For example, an adjoining landowner can sue you for damage to his property caused by your release of pollutants. Such a suit would be the subject of the personal injury pollution exclusion. Under federal and state environmental statutes, environmental regulatory bodies can issue administrative orders requiring you to test for, monitor, and remediate pollutants and pollution. The pollution remediation expense exclusion would apply to these sorts of claims.

Governmental Pollution Damages Claims

Alternately, the environmental regulatory bodies can perform the testing, monitoring, and remediation of pollutants and then sue you to recover the costs of having done so as damages. This variation on the personal injury pollution exclusions is aimed at governmental damages claims in the form of reimbursement for their costs of testing, monitoring, or remediating pollutants.

EXCLUSIONS ADDED BY OTHER INSURERS

Exclusions applicable to the liability and medical payments coverages do not vary widely from insurer to insurer. Some insurers include exclusions for punitive or exemplary damages. In most, but not all, states, punitive damages are not insurable as a matter of law, although there are a few states where there is no such public policy. In those states, if insurers wish to avoid coverage for punitive damages, a specific exclusion for such damages needs to be included.

Some homeowners insurers exclude coverage for claims or suits arising out of the sale or transfer of real property. Such exclusions are intended to make clear that liability coverage does not exist, for example, if an insured is alleged to have concealed the existence of defects or damage from the buyer when the insured sells his or her home.

Chapter 11
Liability Coverage Conditions

As with property coverages, there is a group of conditions applicable to the liability coverage of the homeowners policy. A significant portion of the policy conditions has to do with what the insured must do in the event of a claim or suit. The liability conditions of the ISO HO 2 and HO 3 homeowners policies appear in the policy as follows.

LIMIT OF LIABILITY

This condition provides that the liability coverage limit shown in the policy's declarations is the insurer's total limit for damages in any one occurrence, regardless of the number of: insureds, claims made, or persons insured. This condition further provides that all bodily injury and property damage resulting from one accident or from exposure to the same continuous or repeated conditions will be deemed a single occurrence. Finally, the limit of liability condition provides that the medical payments limit shown in the declarations is the insurer's maximum liability for medical expense for bodily injury for any one person as the result of any one accident.

SEVERABILITY OF INSURANCE

This condition provides that the liability insurance afforded by the policy applies separately as to each insured, but that this condition will not increase the insurer's limit of liability for any one occurrence.

This condition says that the policy must be interpreted separately for each insured against whom a claim is made or a suit may be brought. For example, two persons qualifying as insureds may be named as defendants in a suit seeking bodily injury damages. The event giving rise to the suit may not constitute an accident as to one insured, whereas it does as to the other insured named as a defendant.

A common example is when one insured is sued for an assault or battery and another insured is sued on a vicarious liability theory for the other insured's alleged assault or battery. The conduct on which the suit is based may not be an accident as to the insured committing the assault or battery but may prove to be an accident as to the person sued on a vicarious liability theory. The severability of insurance provision mandates that the insurer evaluate coverage separately for each of the insureds who are sued. In that same example, there may be conflicts of interest between the two defendant insureds that might require that each be represented by separate defense counsel.

In short, this condition means that as to the liability coverage, the availability of liability coverage to an insured and duties owed by and to any insured are independent of the coverage available to and duties owed by and to any other insured.

DUTIES AFTER OCCURRENCE

This condition comprises six subparagraphs. First, the duties after occurrence condition has an introductory paragraph that states that in case of an occurrence, an insured will perform all the duties that apply, and that the insurer will have no obligation to provide coverage if the failure of an insured to perform a required duty prejudices the insurer. (Similar provisions are contained in the liability conditions of personal auto policies and business owners liability coverages.)

Notice Requirement

This duty requires the insured to give written notice to the insurer or the insurer's agent as soon as is practicable after an occurrence. This written notice must include:

- the identity of the policy (the policy number) and the named insured shown on the declaration;
- reasonably available information as to the time, place and circumstances of the occurrence; and,
- the names and addresses of the claimant and witnesses.

Late notice by an insured can be a basis for a denial of coverage. Under the law of most states, an insurer must show that it was prejudiced before it may permissibly deny coverage based on late notice. Usually, this means that the insurer must show that it could have successfully defended against an adverse judgment or could have settled the case for a lesser amount had the insured given timely notice. This is a very high standard to satisfy. Also, many states hold that an insurer cannot assert late notice if the insurer denies coverage on other grounds. The rationale for this latter position is that by denying coverage on other grounds, the insurer has shown that timely notice would not have made a difference in its coverage position.

Cooperation Requirement

This duty requires the insured to cooperate with the insurer in the investigation, settlement, or defense of any claim or suit. This can mean a host of things, depending on the circumstances of a particular case. It includes providing the insurer (and the lawyer hired) with all information and documents in the insured's possession that may be relevant to the defense of the case. It also means assisting counsel in the preparation of and during the lawsuit.

This duty of cooperation means the insured must attend depositions, court hearings, settlement conferences, and trial when requested to do so. It also means giving truthful testimony. One of the important purposes of the cooperation clause is to prevent collusion between the claimant and the insured to the detriment of the insurer.

An insured's breach of his or her duty of cooperation may afford the insurer a basis for denial of coverage. The same high prejudice standard must be satisfied by the insurer before the denial of coverage based on an insured's failure to cooperate will be upheld.

Provide Insurer with All Suit Papers

This duty requires the insured to promptly forward to the insurer every notice, demand, summons, or other process relating to the occurrence. If a lawsuit has not been filed yet, prompt forwarding of a demand may enable the insurer to step in and settle the claim quickly and for much less than might be the case once the litigation has begun. If a lawsuit has been served on you, there is usually a fairly short time before you must enter an appearance in response to service of the lawsuit. Your insurer needs this time to open a claim file, review the complaint, collect pertinent facts, confirm the existence of coverage, reserve rights (if necessary, and inform you of the same), and hire a lawyer to represent you.

If you receive any kind of communication from someone who is claiming damages from you or if you are served with a complaint, call your agent or insurer if it has provided you with a toll-free claim reporting telephone number. Get a copy of any and all documents you receive into your insurer's hands without delay.

Insured's Assistance

This duty specifies some of the things an insured must do to assist in the defense of claims and lawsuits. Think of this condition as an applied example of the duty of cooperation. These duties are:

- ◆ to assist in settling the case (this includes attending mediation and settlement conferences, and executing settlement agreements and other documents necessary to resolve the case);

♦ to assist the insurer in enforcing any right you may have against another person or entity for contribution or indemnity;

♦ to assist in the conduct of suits, including attending hearings and trials; and,

♦ to assist in securing and giving evidence and in obtaining the attendance of witnesses.

Proof of Loss Requirement

This condition relates to the additional coverage for damage to property of others and requires the insured to provide the insurer with a sworn statement of loss within sixty days after the loss. You may also have to show the damaged property to the insurer if the property is in your custody or control.

Voluntary Payment Condition

This is a highly important condition! It provides that the insured may not voluntarily make any payment, assume any obligation, or incur any expense (other than for first aid at the time of bodily injury) on a matter covered by the policy. This condition is designed to protect the insurer's contractual right to control the defense and settlement of claims and lawsuits.

For example, if after being served with a lawsuit, you go out and hire your own lawyer before you tender the defense of the lawsuit to your insurer, the insurer may have no obligation to reimburse you for fees you pay to your lawyer. The same comments apply to cases in which you are sued, hire a lawyer, and defend the case for a period of time before you tender the defense of the lawsuit to your insurer. This could occur if you or your lawyer are acting under a mistake or misapprehension that no coverage would exist or for any other reason.

MEDICAL PAYMENTS COVERAGE

As noted, the medical payments coverage is virtually a no-fault, low-limit bodily injury coverage. In order to be entitled to payment under the medical payments coverage, the injured person must comply with certain requirements. These are to:

- give the insurer written proof of claim, including under oath at the insurer's request, as soon as is practicable;
- authorize the insurer to obtain copies of the injured person's medical records and reports; and,
- submit to physical examination by a doctor of the insurer's choice when and as often as the insurer reasonably requires.

Payment of Claim

This condition provides that payment of benefits under medical payments coverage does not constitute an admission of liability by either the insurer or the insured.

This condition is very important. Many claims handled under the medical payments coverage never evolve into lawsuits. In some cases, however, a lawsuit does follow, often where the injured party's damages exceed the limits of liability of the medical payments coverage. Because of that risk, it would be imprudent for either an insured or an insurer to agree to make a payment under the medical payments coverage. That is, unless it is understood that such a payment does not constitute an admission of liability and cannot be used as evidence by the injured party.

SUITS AGAINST US

This is actually a set of three conditions. The first condition provides that no action can be brought against the insurer unless there has been full compliance with the terms and conditions of the liability coverages. As with the similar property condition, this provision cannot prevent an insured from suing his or her insurer. This provision provides the insurer with the contractual basis for relying on the insured's failure to comply with all the insured's obligations, such as under the notice and voluntary payment provisions, as a defense to the lawsuit.

The second of this set of conditions provides that no one has the right to join the insurer as a party to a lawsuit against any insured. This condition serves two similar purposes. Under the law of most states, evidence that a defendant has insurance that may respond to and pay a judgment is inadmissible in the lawsuit against the insured. Consideration of such evidence could cause a jury to award damages against a defendant when the evidence does not support liability, merely because the dollars to pay the judgment would not be coming directly out of the defendant's pocket.

The third of this set of conditions provide that no action can be brought against the insurer until the insured's obligation to the claimant has been determined by final judgment or settlement agreement that has been signed by the insurer. This condition is intended to protect the insurer from claims in which the claimant and insured have acted in collusion to the detriment of the insurer, as well as the insurer's right to control the defense and settlement of claims and lawsuits.

BANKRUPTCY OF AN INSURED

This provision is required to be included in liability policies in many states. It provides that the bankruptcy or insolvency of an insured will not relieve the insurer of its obligations under the policy. A claimant can seek relief from the automatic stay afforded to a debtor in bankruptcy to continue to press his or her lawsuit against the insured as long as the claimant limits any recovery to proceeds of the insured's insurance policies.

OTHER INSURANCE

This condition addresses the question of which policy should pay, and in what order, when multiple policies afford coverage for the same loss. The ISO

HO 3 homeowners policy purports to provide that the coverage afforded applies in excess of that of any other policy, except for coverage that is written specifically to apply as excess insurance over the ISO HO 3 policy's coverage. In many cases in which there are true conflicts between the other insurance clauses of multiple policies that apply to the same loss, the result is that the insurers are held to share responsibility for the judgment on a pro rata basis. Each shares responsibility in the proportion that the policy limit of the respective insurer's policy bears to the total policy limits of all the involved policies.

Such conflicts between the other insurance clauses in the homeowners policy context are relatively rare. This is an issue that arises far more commonly in the commercial liability context.

POLICY PERIOD

This condition states the policy's coverage applies only to bodily injury or property damage that occurs during the policy period. Under the personal injury coverage endorsement, this condition is deleted as to the personal injury coverage. This is because the trigger of personal injury coverage is the insured's commission of a personal injury offense during the policy period. The personal injury endorsement substitutes a condition that so states.

CONCEALMENT OR FRAUD

This is an important and broad condition that has the effect of voiding the policy completely for *an* insured who, whether before or after a loss, has:

- ◆ intentionally concealed or misrepresented any material fact or circumstance;
- ◆ engaged in fraudulent conduct; or,
- ◆ made false statements relating to the insurance. *Any* false statement or concealment can have the effect of completely voiding the policy.

The concealment or fraud condition of the liability coverage thus differs significantly from that applicable to the property coverages. Under the concealment or fraud condition of the property conditions, the concealment or fraud of one insured will not necessarily void coverage as to other insureds.

PERSONAL INJURY COVERAGE CONDITIONS

The personal injury endorsement has a brief set of conditions. The personal injury endorsement contains limits of liability, severability of insurance, and duties after offense conditions that are substantially identical to their counterparts in the bodily injury and property damage conditions.

CONDITIONS THAT APPLY TO ALL COVERAGES

The concluding section of homeowners policies (before endorsements are attached) consists of policy conditions that apply to both the property and liability (including the medical payments) coverages. These conditions are addressed in the order in which they appear in the ISO HO 3 homeowners policy.

Liberalization Clause

As is included in the current ISO HO 3 homeowners policy, this condition has two parts. The first part is historical and, with varying verbiage, has long been a part of insurance policies. The first part of this condition provides that if the insurer makes a change in coverage that broadens coverage without an additional premium charge, the change will automatically apply as of the date on which the insurer implements the change.

The second portion of the liberalization clause adds a number of qualifications that are largely the product of the consequences of insurers making changes in the policies, some of which arguably may have broadened coverage and others of which may have narrowed coverage.

This part of the clause states that it does not apply to policy changes that are implemented within a general program revision that includes both broadenings and restrictions in coverage. This is true regardless of whether the general program revision is implemented by means of a new edition of the policy or by a mandatory endorsement. This provision is so broad in its sweep that it is difficult to imagine what remains of the original intent of the liberalization clause that has not been subsumed by this new language.

Waiver or Change of Policy Provisions

This condition is pretty straightforward and informs the insured that any waiver or change in the policy's provision must be in writing to be effective. As a general rule, this provision actually helps to prevent misunderstandings and protects the interests of both the insured and the insurer. It limits the ability of either to claim there was an agreement to change policy terms without written evidence of the agreement.

This provision is not ironclad. Agents of an insurer (insurance agents, claim representatives, and attorneys employed by insurers) can and do bind the insurer to changes in the terms of policies. Whether a waiver of a policy provision has occurred as the result of conduct by an agent, employee, or representative of an insurer is a highly fact-dependent inquiry and no general rule can be stated.

The concluding sentence of this condition states that the insurer's demand for appraisal or an examination under oath does not waive any of the insurer's rights. This means that the insurer's investigation of a claim should not be regarded as a waiver of its right to contest coverage if the consequence of its investigation leads the insurer to the conclusion that no coverage for the loss exists. Under the insurance statutes of most states, the insurer must promptly investigate claims and make a claim decision. The fact, for example, that there may be issues as to the amount of a loss may well be independent of the question whether the cause of a loss is covered or whether the property in question constitutes covered property. Thus, an insurer may need to demand appraisal in order to set the amount of a loss even in the case of claims in which the existence of coverage may be questionable. The fact that an insurer demands appraisal when there is a dispute as to the amount of a loss does not, without more, constitute an admission by the insurer that coverage exists.

Similarly, in order to adequately investigate various aspects of a loss, it may be necessary for an insurer to demand an examination under oath of the insured. A potential consequence of an examination under oath may be a partial or total denial of coverage. This provision simply makes clear that by exercising its right to demand an examination under oath, the insurer is not in any way communicating an admission or concession that coverage, in fact, exists.

Cancellation

The cancellation condition in the standard ISO HO 3 homeowners policy is often superseded by specific states' statutory limitations on cancellation. These are typically added to policies by way of state-specific amendatory endorsements because they vary so widely from state to state. However, certain general concepts exist.

To no surprise, failure to pay premiums due for a policy gives the insurer almost unfettered leeway to cancel a policy. Generally, the entire policy premium is payable in advance of the inception date of the policy. Many insurers offer some form of installment payment plan. If you do not pay, coverage lapses. While an insurer may reinstate coverage once it receives a late premium payment, it usually only does so prospectively, not retrospectively. If you have a loss during the period when coverage lapsed and was cancelled due to nonpayment, you are out of luck. This is not a gamble you want to take. Pay your premiums and pay them timely.

Nonrenewal

The ISO HO 3 homeowners policy's nonrenewal condition provides that the insurer may decide not to renew coverage on expiration of the policy. If it chooses to do so, it must give the insured at least thirty days written notice of its intent not to renew prior to the expiration date. As with the cancellation condition, many states place different limits on an insurer's right to not renew homeowners policies.

Assignment

This condition provides that the insured may not assign the policy without the insurer's consent. It recognizes that an insurance policy is a personal contract between the insurer and the insured. The insurer has the right to decide who it will and will not insure. The assignment protects that right. This is a standard condition that applies in one form or another in essentially all insurance policies, not just homeowners policies.

Subrogation

When a property insurer pays for a loss to covered property, the insurer becomes subrogated to, or succeeds to, the rights of the insured against any third party who may have been responsible for causing the loss. This right of subrogation arises as a matter of law. It prevents an insured from a double recovery, that is, recovery both under the policy and recovery in damages from the person who caused the loss. When an insurer makes a recovery against the responsible party, that operates to help make the insurer whole for its payment of the loss.

The subrogation condition first acknowledges that the insured may waive all rights of recovery against a third party prior to the occurrence of a loss. The subrogation condition next provides that if the insured has not entered into such a waiver, the insurer may require that the insured assign its rights of recovery against a third party to the extent the insurer has paid the insured's loss.

Third, the subrogation condition requires that when the insurer demands such an assignment of rights against a third party by the insured, the insured must sign and deliver all related papers and must cooperate with the insurer. That means, for example, that if the insurer must sue the third party and call the insured as a witness, the insured must cooperate and appear.

Chapter 12
Choosing Liability Limits

Liability coverages under homeowners' policies are commonly offered at the following levels, all on a per-occurrence basis: $100,000; $300,000; $500,000; and $1,000,000. If a person wishes to purchase liability coverage with limits in excess of $1,000,00 per occurrence, he or she must often purchase a separate, personal liability umbrella policy.

Annual premiums charged for higher liability limits are usually quite modest. In light of the relatively low cost of increased liability limits and the magnitude of potential jury verdicts that can result in today's world, the average person should not purchase less than $500,000 in liability limits as part of his or her homeowners policy. Limits of $100,000 and $300,000 simply do not afford sufficient protection in the event of a serious loss.

A good way of helping you to decide how much to purchase in liability limits is to assess the value of your assets—in other words, how much are you at risk of losing? In several major urban areas, the average value of many middle-class families' homes exceeds $300,000. Many insureds would be surprised at the resulting figures if they were to conduct a complete inventory of their possessions to total what it would cost to replace all of them.

When you envision the value of your home, personal possessions, and savings, you can readily see the need for substantial liability limits. The greater your liability limits, the more protection afforded from a judgment creditor's attempt to seize your assets to satisfy a judgment.

In the commercial liability insurance business, risk managers for insured companies, their agents or brokers, and the underwriters for insurance companies often refer to high level excess liability policies as sleep insurance. This means that the company management and shareholders of the insured need not lose sleep over the possibility that a catastrophic loss might exceed the company's liability insurance limits and thereby potentially threaten or impair the future financial liability of the company.

The same concept applies to individuals. It is preferable to have the peace of mind that comes with the knowledge that you have taken reasonable and prudent steps to obtain the financial security and protection that comes with paying a small amount of additional premium for increased liability insurance limits.

For example, the annual personal umbrella liability policy premium, covering three cars and a homeowners policy, with limits of $1.5 million, can be found for a little over $300 annually, applying over a $500,000 homeowner's liability limit and a $250,000 per person/$500,000 per accident auto liability limit.

If you purchase higher liability limits on your homeowners policy (and auto policy), the premiums for a personal umbrella policy will be reduced. This is because as the limits of the underlying policies are higher, the personal liability umbrella policy insurer's exposure to loss is lower.

STRUCTURING YOUR LIABILITY INSURANCE LIMITS

Deciding on how to structure your liability insurance limits depends on who your insurer is and the limits of liability the insurer is willing to write under a homeowners policy for personal liability. There are two basic approaches to the problem. One approach is to purchase a moderately high liability limit with your homeowners policy, such as $300,000 or $500,000, and purchase a separate personal liability umbrella policy with a limit of $1,000,000 or $2,000,000 (depending on your needs) to apply in excess of the homeowners policy liability limits. The benefit to the personal umbrella liability approach is that the personal umbrella liability policy's limits of liability will also apply in excess of your auto liability policy's liability limits. For many persons, their exposure to a large liability loss arising out of their use of the car or truck is substantially greater than that arising from the ownership or maintenance of their home.

The other approach is to purchase the maximum available liability limit on your homeowners policy alone, assuming your insurer will write policies with liability limits of at least $1,000,000. Usually, but not always, purchasing moderate homeowners liability limits of $300,000 or $500,000, plus the personal umbrella policy with limits of at least $1,000,000, will be more economical from a premium standpoint.

Insurers also differ in their underwriting approach. Some insurers do not offer personal umbrella policies, with the result that your agent will have to procure a personal umbrella from an insurer other than your homeowners or auto insurer. Other insurers offer personal umbrella policies, but not to insureds who have their homeowners and auto policies with that same insurer.

The issue here is the concept of *pyramiding of risk*. Some insurers simply do not want to commit to that much exposure for loss with respect to any one insured. Insurers that take this view are often willing to be either the primary (*i.e.*, the homeowners liability insurer) or the excess (*i.e.*, the personal umbrella policy) liability insurer, but not both.

Other insurers take the opposite view, particularly in the personal lines context. These insurers would rather be both the primary and excess insurer for the same insured (particularly when the insured has both his or her auto and homeowners insurance with the same insurer). Insurers that hold this view usually cite the fact that they are getting greater premiums and have complete control over a major claim, eliminating the need to deal with another insurer's claim department.

Disagreements can often arise between the primary (homeowner's) insurer's claim department and the excess insurer's (the personal umbrella policy) claim department over defense and settlement strategy in the event of a claim that presents a potential for penetrating the personal umbrella policy insurer's coverage. What often happens is that the primary insurer believes the case has a settlement value in excess of its policy limits and wants the umbrella insurer to contribute some money in order to settle the case. The umbrella insurer, which is not exposed to the ongoing cost of defending the suit and which therefore does not have that financial pressure on it, will take a hard line, asserting that the genuine settlement value of the case is within the primary insurer's limits, and will refuse to contribute to the settlement. When this occurs, cases can be forced to trial that ought to be settled, and can sometimes result in runaway verdicts that exceed the limits of both the primary and the excess insurance policies.

There is yet another reason why a personal umbrella policy should be part of your basic package of insurance policies. While personal umbrella policies have their own terms, conditions, and exclusions, they provide an important *gap-filling* function. The usual personal umbrella policy insuring agreement provides that the personal umbrella insurer does not have a duty to defend— a duty that your homeowner's or auto liability insurer has. Except—and this is the important exception—your personal umbrella policy insurer has a duty to defend a suit against you seeking damages within the personal umbrella policy's coverage that are not covered under the underlying policies.

An easy example of how this might work is if the liability coverage of your homeowners policy does not include personal injury coverage. For things such as libel, slander, false arrest, false imprisonment, etc., your personal umbrella policy (in most cases) will provide coverage.

In short, a personal umbrella policy is something that provides a substantial amount of coverage at a modest price. The basic recommendation of a minimum qualifying homeowner's and auto liability limit and over $1,000,000 personal umbrella policy is just the starting point. Each individual needs to assess his or her own needs and to determine what protection limit he or she believes is appropriate. Increasing liability limits over the minimum is usually not very expensive under either a homeowners or auto policy. Nor is increasing liability limits of $1.5 million or $2 million under personal umbrella policies. Each situation will differ. The cost of personal umbrella policies are often affected more by the auto liability exposures you present. A family with more vehicles and drivers can expect to be charged more than one with fewer vehicles and drivers.

PART III: Your Auto

Chapter 13

Personal Automobile Policies

Many insureds face a greater risk of incurring an insurable loss arising out of their use of cars and trucks than out of their ownership and use of their home. Cars and trucks travel at high speeds on roads in close proximity to other vehicles. When collisions occur, there is naturally a great risk of serious property damage or bodily injury.

Like homeowners policies, auto policies include both first-party coverages (*i.e.,* coverage for physical damage to *your* car or truck) and third-party coverages (*i.e.,* coverage for your liability for damages to *others*). In addition, depending on the jurisdiction, uninsured or underinsured motorist coverage or both may be required as part of the personal auto policy. These coverages provide protection for you if you are involved in an accident that is the fault of another driver and he or she either does not have liability insurance or has liability insurance with limits that are not sufficient to cover your damages.

Finally, in a limited number of jurisdictions, drivers must carry *no-fault policies*. No-fault auto insurance was intended to speed up the resolution of smaller claims and to lessen the number of personal injury lawsuits arising from less serious collisions.

At present, there are twelve no-fault states. They are:

 ◆ District of Columbia
 ◆ Florida

- Hawaii
- Kansas
- Kentucky
- Massachusetts
- Michigan
- Minnesota
- New Jersey
- New York
- North Dakota
- Pennsylvania
- Utah

In addition, there are several other states where no-fault (formally known as *personal injury protection*) coverage is an optional coverage.

If you live in one of the twelve mandatory no-fault states, you will need to learn about your state's specific requirements. Even in these twelve mandatory no-fault states, the coverages and required minimum coverage limits vary. In addition, whether an insurer can *opt out* of no-fault coverage and the limits of injury or damage at which the no-fault benefits no longer apply vary from state to state. When an accident results in damages in excess of a given state's mandatory no fault limits, the injured person retains the right to sue for damages.

To complicate matters further, there are a few states where personal injury protection coverage can be purchased as an optional coverage. As a practical matter, the laws in many of these states overlap significantly with several of the states where no-fault coverage is nominally mandatory.

Because the no-fault laws vary so much from state to state, it is beyond the scope of this book to do other than to highlight the need to understand your state's no-fault laws and to govern your purchase of coverage limits accordingly.

In addition, there is overlap between uninsured motorist and underinsured motorist coverage, and personal injury coverage. Thus, in an optional personal injury protection jurisdiction, a person needs to carefully consider the pros and cons of increased uninsured motorist and underinsured motorist coverage as opposed to purchasing increased limits of personal injury protection coverage.

All states have some form of financial responsibility laws under which a person is not allowed to register a car or a truck without having provided proof of statutorily-mandated minimum levels of bodily injury and property damage liability insurance. Correspondingly, insurers in each of the states sell *statutory limit* liability policies that permit a person to satisfy his or her state's financial responsibility laws to be able to register his or her car or truck. These minimum financial responsibility law requirements are usually very low—too low, in fact. They are not remotely sufficient given current auto prices, costs of repair, and medical and health care costs.

STRUCTURE OF PERSONAL AUTO POLICIES

As with homeowners policies, there is a standard personal auto policy published by the Insurance Services Office. As is the case with homeowners policies, many insurers, particularly direct writers such as State Farm, Allstate, and Farmers, use proprietary policy forms for their personal auto policies. Furthermore, jurisdictions, like Massachusetts, have established a statutorily-mandated personal auto policy. The provisions of the standard ISO personal auto policy and of the proprietary policies sold by other insurers tend to be more alike in their basic coverage provisions than they differ.

Coverage provisions in the ISO personal auto policy are grouped as follows:

- definitions;
- liability coverages;
- medical payments coverage;
- uninsured motorist coverage;
- first-party physical damage coverages;
- insured's duties after accident or loss; and,
- general provisions.

Proprietary personal auto policy forms used by insurers that do not employ the ISO personal auto policy forms may differ in the order in which these categories of provisions appear. Personal auto policies issued in no-fault states also differ from the ISO personal auto policy. For example, the Massachusetts Automobile Insurance Policy first lists the policy's definition and the four compulsory coverages, which include the no-fault coverages. Following the basic coverage provisions are the optional coverage provisions. These are then followed by the general provisions and exclusions, with provisions relating to cancellation and renewal, the insured's duties in case of accident or loss, and the safe driver insurance plan provisions.

INSURABLE INTEREST

Before discussing the actual provisions of auto policies, the concepts of insurable interest and insured capacity, as they relate to the coverages afforded by auto policies, should be discussed. As with homeowners policies, the concept of *insurable interest* relates to the coverages for physical damage to your auto. A person must have an insurable interest in the auto in question to be entitled to payment of a loss. The easy insurable interest concepts are those of the registered owner and a lien holder, such as your auto loan lender or leasing company of a covered vehicle. However, coverage also extends to nonowned autos. The common definitions of *nonowned autos* includes rental vehicles and borrowed vehicles as long as they are not regularly available for use by a named insured or a family member.

Spouses will generally be considered to have an insurable interest even if not a registered owner of the vehicle.

The concept of *insured capacity* is mostly a question of the definitions of *insured*, *covered person*, *family member*, or *eligible injured person*, as well as those arising under the vehicle codes and other state laws. For example, the laws of a particular state may require that a person using a vehicle with the named insured's express or implied permission be covered as an insured under the named insured's policy. Such requirements are related to the named insured's statutory liability as the vehicle owner for bodily injury or property damage arising out of its use.

PERSONAL AUTO POLICY DEFINITIONS

Common definitions used in the ISO personal auto policy form include the following.

Accident

The ISO personal auto policy uses the terms *auto accident*, *accident*, and *accidental*, without specifically defining any of those terms. Many of the policy forms used by insurers that do not employ the ISO personal auto policy do define *accident*. Most such definitions incorporate some form of *unexpected* or *unintended* language. This is to make clear the fundamental concept that insurance applies only to fortuitous losses, not to expected or intended losses.

Bodily Injury

Bodily Injury means bodily harm, sickness, or disease, including death that results. This is essentially the same as the bodily injury definition of the ISO HO 3 homeowners policy's liability coverage. Occasional variations are seen in other policies, but this is a standard and workable definition. (However, the Massachusetts Auto Insurance Policy does not contain a definition of bodily injury at all.)

Business

Business includes trade, profession or occupation. Not all personal auto policies contain a definition of business.

Family Member

Family member means a person related to you by blood, marriage, or adoption who is a resident of your household. This includes a ward or foster child. Other insurers' definitions can add qualifications that eliminate coverage for wards or foster children or for children who have manifested an intent to reside elsewhere permanently. Where you need to be careful is if you have children who reside temporarily elsewhere because they are attending school or are in the military, but whose legal address is still your residence. You need to assure that your policy's definition of family member extends to your children in such a situation in order to assure that they continue to qualify as insureds under your policy. If the definition of family member does not extend to such circumstances, then it may be necessary to obtain a separate policy to cover your child's use of vehicles while temporarily away at school or in the military. (The Massachusetts Auto Insurance Policy contains a definition of *household member* that is substantially the same as the definition of family member in the ISO personal auto policy.)

Occupying

Occupying means in, upon, or getting in, on, out, or off. This definition relates to a very important concept applicable to auto liability insurance. Historically, the insuring agreements of many auto policies stated in substance and effect that coverage applied to liability arising out of the ownership, maintenance, or use of covered autos. Over the decades, there has been an enormous amount of litigation over what constitutes *ownership, maintenance, or use* of covered autos. Occupying will be discussed in greater detail in the discussion on liability coverages of auto policies. (see Chapter 14.) Suffice it to say for now that the concept of occupying a covered auto is one that relates to what constitutes *ownership, maintenance, or use* of covered autos.

Property Damage

Property damage means physical injury to tangible property, including its loss of use. This is essentially the same definition as appears in homeowner's liability coverage. The discussion of the property damage definitions of homeowners policies also applies to the concept of property damage under auto liability coverages. (The Massachusetts Auto Insurance Policy does not contain a definition of property damage.)

Trailer

There are two concepts that are important to understand with respect to this definition. First, *trailers* are vehicles that are designed to be towed by private passenger autos, pickup trucks, vans, or other similar vehicles designed for use on public roads. This also includes farm wagons and implements when towed by one of the above categories of vehicles.

Second, *trailers* are deemed to be covered vehicles for purposes of the policies' liability coverages. In the policies of insurers that do not use the ISO form, these concepts are likely to be included, but they may appear within the policies in other locations or under other headings.

Your Covered Auto

The concepts embraced by this definition contained in the ISO personal auto policy are relatively complex. Most of these concepts appear in one form or another in the policies of insurers that do not use the ISO form. Again, check your own policy to confirm whether these provisions are included. The complexity of the definition reflects the increasing complexity of modern life and reflects insurers' attempts to make clear for their customers what loss exposures are and are not covered. Some of the complexities in this definition also correspond to statutory requirements under states' vehicle and insurance codes.

The first subcategory under this definition is *any vehicles shown in the policy's declarations*. However, when more than one policy may apply to a particular loss, confusion can occur. Since it is common in the case of auto accidents that more than one policy may apply to the same loss, there are rules for determining which policy applies. Often these rules are statutory, and thus can vary from state to state. An almost universal rule, however, is the rule that states that the policy in which an insured vehicle is specifically rated or described always applies to the loss first.

The next category of covered autos includes private passenger autos, pickup trucks, or vans that have gross vehicle weights of less than 10,000 pounds. This provision has many qualifications. First, the insured must acquire the vehicle during the policy period. Second, the insured must report the acquisition of the vehicle to the insurer within thirty days after the insured acquires it. Third, pickup trucks or vans do not qualify if any other policies afford coverage for those vehicles.

These latter qualifications mean that small installation or repair contractors and farmers who purchase pickups or vans that are comparable to those that people purchase for ordinary personal use can cover their business- or work-related use of such vehicles under their personal auto policy. This is available for those people whose business use is not so extensive as to require a commercial auto policy.

This provision of your auto policy makes clear that you get automatic coverage for newly acquired vehicles. However, such automatic coverage only applies for thirty days and only if you actually report the acquisition to your insurer within the thirty-day period. If you take the responsibility for reporting your acquisition of a new vehicle to your agent, you will minimize the risk of a gap in coverage that could result if the dealership's finance department fails to timely notify your insurer.

There are a couple of other qualifications to this *newly acquired* auto coverage provision. If the newly acquired vehicle is a replacement for a covered vehicle described in the policy's declarations *and* you report the new vehicle within thirty days of its acquisition, the coverages that applied to the former vehicle will apply to the newly acquired vehicle. Further, if the new vehicle is a *new vehicle* in the absolute sense, that is, the vehicle is not replacing an existing vehicle, this new vehicle is automatically covered and it will be covered to the broadest extent of any existing covered vehicle under the policy.

Your covered vehicle also includes any car, truck, or trailer that you rent or use as a temporary substitute vehicle if you are out of your normal vehicle because of:

- breakdown;
- repair;
- servicing;
- loss; or,
- destruction.

In practical terms, this means that if you borrow or rent a vehicle while your car is unavailable to you because of any of these circumstances, you are covered for use of that substitute vehicle. In other words, if your car breaks down or even is in the shop or dealership for normal maintenance work, you are covered for use of:

- a friend's or neighbor's vehicle;
- a rented vehicle; or,
- a loaner vehicle while yours is in the shop.

The definitions of the concepts of your covered auto in proprietary policy forms used by insurers that do not use the ISO personal auto policy form can be more restrictive or more liberal than these definitions. Some insurers place lower gross vehicle weight limits on this coverage, effectively limiting coverage to private passenger cars and effectively excluding most SUVs, vans, and many full-size pick-up trucks. Other companies do not include any sort of gross vehicle weight limitation in the definition of your covered auto. (The Massachusetts Automobile Insurance Policy incorporates the same 10,000 pound gross vehicle weight limit as does the ISO policy.)

LIABILITY COVERAGE PROVISIONS

The insuring agreement of the liability coverage of the ISO personal auto liability provides that the insurer will pay for damages for bodily injury or property damage for which any *insured* becomes responsible because of an auto accident. The insuring agreement provides that the insurer will settle or defend as it deems appropriate any claim or suit seeking such damages. The insuring agreement provides that the insurer's duty to defend terminates when the policy limit has been exhausted.

Supplemental Payments

As with the liability coverage of the homeowners policies, the auto liability coverage of the ISO personal auto policy includes several coverages under the heading *Supplementary Payments*. These are substantially similar to the supplementary payments coverages of homeowners policies, but are not identical to them.

These supplementary payments coverages include:

- up to $250 for the cost of bail bonds required because of an accident, including related traffic law violations, provided the action results in covered bodily injury or property damage;

- premiums for appeal bonds and bonds to release attachments in suits that the insurer defends;

- postjudgment interest on that portion of a judgment against an insured that is within the policy limits of the policy (postjudgment interest is covered from the time of entry of judgment until the time the insurer offers to pay that portion of the judgment that is within the policy limits);

- up to $50 per day for loss of earnings—but not other forms of income—because of attendance at hearings or trials at the request of the insurer (often, insurers will pay greater per diem amounts for attendance at hearings or trials, when the insured can show that his or her lost wages exceed that amount and the insured has an actual loss of income (*i.e.,* his or her employer does not pay the insured for the time off work));

- other reasonable expenses incurred by the insured at the insurer's request; and,

- expenses for emergency first aid to others at an accident involving an auto covered by the policy.

The supplementary payments provisions of insurers that do not use the ISO personal auto policy and the Massachusetts Automobile Insurance Policy usually are substantially similar, differing principally in the daily amount payable for lost earnings and premiums payable for bail bonds.

Choosing Liability Limits

In the auto liability context, the need to purchase increased liability limits is even more important than it is in the homeowner's liability context. Average vehicle costs and costs to repair vehicles are much higher than they were in the past. It is not uncommon for persons to drive vehicles whose new purchase prices exceed $30,000, $40,000, or even $50,000. Generally, the more expensive a vehicle is to purchase, the more expensive it is to repair. Plus, not every collision involves just two vehicles. Take a moment and consider your potential liability if *you* are determined to have been at fault, or primarily at fault, for a multi-vehicle pile up.

Similar comments apply to your potential liability for injury to persons. That liability can include not only the costs of their medical treatment, but also the costs of their loss of income during the period they are unable to work.

For these reasons and those discussed in connection with homeowners policies, the absolute minimum limits that the average person should carry in terms of liability limits on his or her auto liability coverage are:

- ◆ $50,000 property damage per accident;
- ◆ $100,000 per person/$300,000 per accident bodily injury; *and*,
- ◆ at least a $1,000,000 personal umbrella policy.

Persons with greater income or assets should seriously consider purchasing significantly higher limits.

Chapter 14
Auto Liability Coverage Exclusions

Because cars and trucks are by nature mobile, the liability coverages of personal auto policies do not draw the hard or consistent distinctions between liability arising out of personal activities and liability arising out of business activities that homeowner liability coverages do. However, there are some similarities.

Personal auto liability policies exclude coverage for categories of business use of cars and trucks that are more properly the subject of commercial auto policies. These categories include trucking and delivery companies, companies that transport people for hire, auto dealers, auto repair businesses, commercial garages, among others.

FAMILY MEMBERS

An almost universal exclusion in personal automobile policies is one that excludes coverage for bodily injury to the named insured or family members. There are a number of reasons why such exclusions are included in auto liability policies. One is the risk of collusion between or among family members that could lead to fraudulent or inflated damages claims. Rather, injury to the named insured and family members is covered, but under the medical payments coverage, with its lower limits, not the liability coverages. A few states prohibit such family member exclusions, but they are a decided minority.

This manner of structuring these coverages also recognizes the fact that most persons have medical insurance, if not also disability insurance. Often, such agreements have provisions requiring the insured to reimburse the health plan to the extent they obtain recovery from other sources of insurance. Such provisions are common and need to be understood and contemplated, especially before a person enters into a contingent fee retainer agreement with an attorney.

The average person needs to understand that typically the attorney's contingent fee does not include any *costs* of litigation. The fee is calculated on the basis of the gross amount of a settlement or judgment, regardless of any contractual indemnity or reimbursement obligations the insured may have under a health insurance plan. Thus, if an insured retains an attorney after an accident on a contingent fee basis, the fee does not include costs or liens that a health insurer or workers compensation insurer may have against the ultimate recovery. After the attorney's fee is deducted and costs are paid, the insured could find him- or herself in the position of owing money to reimburse a workers compensation or health insurer and have no net recovery from the personal injury suit.

INTENTIONAL INJURY OR DAMAGE

The ISO personal automobile policy's liability coverage precludes coverage for any insured who intentionally causes bodily injury or property damage. The manner in which this exclusion is worded is somewhat narrower than the *intentional acts* exclusion of homeowner's liability coverage.

The focus of the intentional acts exclusion of homeowners policies is the insured's intent to commit the act that results in bodily injury or property damage, regardless of whether the insured intended bodily injury or property damage to result. The automobile liability intentional acts exclusion is narrower, because its focus is on the insured's intent to commit the bodily injury or property damage that resulted.

OWNED OR TRANSPORTED PROPERTY

This exclusion precludes coverage for property damage to property owned or being transported by the insured. The purpose of this exclusion is to assure that the correct policy or coverage applies to a given element of loss.

The injury or damage to the insured's vehicle is covered under the automobile physical damage portion of the policy. Injury or damage to an insured's personal property that is the result of an auto accident should be covered under the personal property coverage of the insured's homeowners policy. Injury or damage to personal property of another that the insured was transporting again would be the subject of homeowners policy coverages.

RENTED, USED, OR CARED-FOR PROPERTY

This exclusion precludes coverage for property damage to property rented to, used by, or in the care of an insured, and has an exception for property damage to a residence or a garage. The intent of auto policies is to afford coverage for rented or borrowed vehicles under the policy's first-party physical damage coverage, not the liability coverage. As to personal property that is rented to, used by, or in the care of the insured that is damaged in an auto accident, this exclusion makes clear that it is the insured's homeowners coverages that should apply.

Finally, the exception contained in this exclusion for property damage to residences or private garages rented by, used by, or in the care of an insured recognizes that coverage should exist if you damage a residence or garage by colliding with it while operating your car or truck. This is a type of loss that is within the normal expectations of liability coverage arising out of your use of an automobile—you hit something and damage it, creating liability that your insurance should cover.

BODILY INJURY TO INSURED'S EMPLOYEES

This exclusion is comparable to that contained in the homeowners policies. It precludes coverage for bodily injury to employees of the insured that occur within the course of employment. There is an exception to this exclusion—it does not apply unless workers compensation benefits are required or are available for that employee for that injury.

In practical terms, this means that if you live in a state where persons are required to provide workers compensation insurance for domestic employees, your homeowners policy is likely to include an *additional coverage* for that obligation. Thus, this exposure to loss is intended to be covered by the workers compensation additional coverage of your homeowners policy, even if the injury in question arises out of your use of personal vehicles.

If you are required to have workers compensation coverage and do not, then the exception to this exclusion applies, with the result that you will be covered for such a loss.

PUBLIC OR LIVERY CONVEYANCES

This exclusion precludes coverage for the insured's liability arising out of the ownership or operation of a vehicle while it is being used as a public or livery conveyance. This exclusion has an exception for shared expense carpools.

It is important to understand the purposes of this exclusion and just how far it reaches. The basic intent is pretty clear—you are not covered under personal auto liability coverage for bodily injury or property damage arising out of a public or livery conveyance business. This is one example in which the standard auto policy does not necessarily make itself clear. *Public conveyance* or *livery conveyance* are terms of art. They refer to the transporting of both property and persons for hire. Thus, this exclusion embraces trucking and delivery operations, as well as taxicab, airport shuttle, and car service operations. There are complex state and federal laws governing these types of businesses. They require a commercial automobile policy. If, however, an accident arose out of personal, nonbusiness use of the vehicle in question, the insured would have coverage. Likewise, if the insured lent the vehicle to a third party who was in an accident while using the vehicle for nonbusiness purposes, the insured owner would still have coverage for his or her statutory owner's liability or his or her liability imposed on a negligent entrustment basis.

As opposed to public or livery conveyance operations, you are covered if you are a participant in a shared expense carpool arrangement. The difference between these two situations is that a public or livery conveyance operation is one conducted for a profit motive. Participation in a shared expense carpool arrangement is usually done for reasons of personal convenience or cost savings, not for a profit motive.

AUTO BUSINESS EXPOSURES

The next exclusion common to personal auto policies is for liability arising out of various categories of auto-related businesses *other than* transportation of property or persons. This exclusion precludes coverage for any insured while employed or otherwise engaged in the *business* of selling, repairing, servicing, storing, or parking vehicles designed for use mainly on public highways. This exclusion includes an exception for the named insured's family member, partner, agent, or employee.

The intent of this exclusion again is to preclude coverage under a personal auto policy for use of cars or trucks of others by persons employed in these types of auto-related businesses. The intent is that coverage for accidents arising out of such use of vehicles should be the subject of an auto dealer's or garagekeeper's liability policies. The exception to the exclusion recognizes the need for coverage for the insured's or family member's use of personally owned vehicles. This includes connection with business use as well as the need for coverage if a personal vehicle is lent to a partner or employee of an auto-related business. This exception exists due to the vehicle owner's statutory liability under state financial responsibility laws.

MAINTENANCE OR USE OF VEHICLES IN BUSINESS CONTEXT

This is a belt-and-suspenders exclusion intended to fill gaps in the previous two exclusions. This exclusion precludes coverage for maintenance or use of any vehicle while the insured is employed or otherwise engaged in any business that is not one of the auto-related businesses described in the previous exclusion. However, this exclusion precludes coverage for your maintenance or use of an employer-provided vehicle while used for business or employment activities. For example, if you company-provided car is in the shop, your employer's commercial auto coverage should apply to a rental.

USE OF VEHICLES WITHOUT PERMISSION

This is one of the most important exclusions applicable to auto liability coverages. It states:

> *We do not provide Liability Coverage for any "insured"...Using a vehicle without a reasonable belief that the "insured" is entitled to do so.*

Far too many persons are far too casual about the extent to which they allow others' use of their vehicles without an appreciation for the liability exposures they are assuming by doing so. This exclusion is not going to put a vehicle owner on the hook for a carjacker's injuries inflicted on others after he or she steals your car or truck. It could, however, limit your coverage if a child or other person uses your car or truck in a manner beyond your expected reasonable permission to them for use of that vehicle.

For example, your son or daughter may have your permission to use your car or truck, but that grant of permissible use does not extend to situations in which they turn over the keys to one of their acquaintances. In such a circumstance, you may only be covered for your state's minimum statutory owner's liability if an accident results.

Because there is serious potential to be uninsured or underinsured due to ambiguities in your granting permission to others to use your vehicle, it is extremely important that the scope and limits of others' permissible use of covered vehicles be made clear before you authorize such use.

NUCLEAR PERIL

As discussed with other coverages, the risk of loss by any peril that would be covered under a policy covering nuclear perils (radiation or radioactivity) is excluded.

MOTORCYCLES AND OFF-ROAD VEHICLES

This exclusion should come as no surprise being under a personal automobile liability policy. This exclusion precludes coverage for:

- vehicles with less than four wheels;
- vehicles designed mainly for use off public roads;
- vehicles other than *your covered auto* that you own or that are regularly available for your use;
- vehicles owned by any family member or are regularly available for your use; or,
- vehicles located within a facility designed for racing or practicing for racing or competition.

Your personal auto policy does not cover loss exposures that you need to separately insure, like your ownership and use of motorcycles, ATVs, or other off-road vehicles. The risks of loss from the use of such other categories of vehicles is greater than that posed by the use of autos. They are inherently more hazardous, even when operated prudently.

OTHER EXCLUSIONS

The ISO personal auto policy, as well as essentially all other policies issued in the United States, contains a nuclear exclusion. As you should have gathered by now, exposures to loss resulting from the risk of war, nuclear explosion, or contamination are standard exclusions.

OTHER COMMENTS

The policies of insurers that do not use the ISO form often include an express exclusion from coverage for punitive damages and the costs of defending claims for punitive damage. Such exclusions are often added by endorsements in certain states where a given insurer's basic auto liability policy does not exclude coverage for punitive damages. Such punitive damages exclusions are wise and fair. In most jurisdictions, punitive damages are not insurable as a matter of public policy, so the exclusion merely acts as a restatement of the law. Nonetheless, that restatement puts the issue into sharp focus and puts the insured on notice that he or she is not covered for such potential losses. This is even more important in those few states where, absent an exclusion, there is no public policy bar against insuring punitive damages.

Chapter 15
Auto Liability Coverage Conditions

While auto policies contain fairly extensive conditions, there is only a short section of provisions applicable specifically to auto liability coverages.

LIMIT OF LIABILITY

The ISO personal auto policy limit of liability condition is quite simple. It provides that the per accident limit of liability shown in the policy's declarations is the most the insurer will pay regardless of the number of insureds, claims made, vehicles or premiums shown in the declarations, or vehicles involved in an accident.

This is one example of an *antistacking* provision. Plaintiffs' personal injury lawyers seeking to maximize recoveries for their clients will commonly urge that the various coverages of *all* applicable coverages should apply. This would increase their clients' settlement leverages and potential recoveries in the event the cases are tried and go to judgment. Because of this, most auto insurance policies include a variety of provisions intended to negate such claims that the limits of various coverages should be *stacked*.

Other insurers' policies sometimes go further. For example, in states where a spouse's *loss of consortium* claim is deemed separate from that of the injured person, only that state's applicable minimum financial responsibility limits are covered for the loss of consortium claim.

Exclusions of this sort mean if the law of your state deems a loss of consortium claim by a spouse to be an independent claim from that of the injured spouse, a separate full policy limit will not apply to the loss of consortium claim. Rather, additional coverage for that loss of consortium claim is limited to the statutory financial responsibility limits that apply in that state (which, depending on the state in question, can be as low as $15,000 per accident).

OUT-OF-STATE COVERAGE

This is a necessary provision in light of the fact that cars and trucks are by definition mobile, creating the risk of injury or damage to others when cars or trucks are used outside the state of the insured's residence. This condition recognizes that the various states' laws as to minimum statutory financial responsibility limits vary, and provides that the policy will conform to the requirements of applicable laws, regardless of the state in which an accident occurs.

This condition provides that if an auto accident occurs in a state or province other than that where your insured vehicle is principally garaged, and the minimum financial responsibility laws of that state or province require a higher bodily injury or property damage limit than those shown in the policy's declarations, the policy will provide the higher limit required by that state or province. This condition is likely to be of concern only to those persons who maintain the minimum limits required.

The second subparagraph of this condition provides that if the state where the accident takes place has laws that require nonresidents operating vehicles within that state to maintain insurance, the policy will provide at least the minimum limits required by that statute's laws.

The final subparagraph of this condition makes clear that this provision will not entitle any person to duplicate payments for the same loss.

FINANCIAL RESPONSIBILITY

This condition is substantially similar to the out-of-state coverage condition. The difference is that this condition is a conformity with the statute provision with respect to the minimum financial responsibility requirements of any state, including the state where a vehicle is principally garaged. It provides that where the insurer certifies the policy as proof of financial responsibility, the policy will afford at least that state's minimum financial responsibility limits.

OTHER INSURANCE

In the auto liability context, it is relatively common for an insured who is involved in an accident to have coverage under more than one policy. Such circumstances arise when the insured is involved in an accident while using a borrowed or rented vehicle, or using a personal vehicle while engaged in employment.

The other insurance provisions of the ISO personal automobile policy provide that if there is other applicable insurance, the coverage of the policy will apply on a shared basis with the other insurance—the limit the policy bears in proportion to the total limit of all the policies. This is made subject to an exception when the vehicle involved is not owned by the insured. In such circumstances, the policy's limits will apply as excess coverage over any other collectible insurance.

There is common provision in policies issued by companies that do not use the ISO personal auto policy. It states that when an insured is covered under more than one policy issued by the same insurer, the total limits of liability available will not exceed the limits of the policy that has the highest limits. This is an example of an antistacking of policy limits provision.

Chapter 16

Medical Payments Coverage

The medical payments coverage of personal auto policies are very similar to those of homeowners policies. This coverage is essentially a low-limit, no-fault coverage that applies to bodily injury claims arising out of use of covered vehicles. The limits of automobile medical payments coverage under most personal automobile policies are only a few thousand dollars. $5,000 is a common limit; $10,000 is sometimes seen.

Auto medical payments provisions often provide for coordination between policies for certain things. These things include the coordination of benefits payable with other benefits available to the insured person, such as workers compensation, or proceeds of insurance policies of other persons who may also have been involved in the accident and who are legally responsible for the injured person's injuries.

The ISO personal automobile policy medical payments insuring agreement provides that the insurer will pay reasonable medical and funeral expenses because of bodily injury caused by an accident and sustained by an insured. Coverage applies for expenses incurred within three years of the date of the accident.

Insured, for purposes of the automobile medical payments coverage, includes the named insured and any family member while occupying a motor vehicle designed for use principally on public roads. It also includes a pedestrian struck by such a vehicle while it is occupied by an insured, and *any other person* while occupying your covered auto.

Since the auto medical payments coverage applies to the named insured and family members while occupying covered vehicles, the medical payments coverage is a first-party coverage. Insofar as coverage extends to two categories of other persons, pedestrians struck by and any other person while occupying your covered auto, the medical payments coverage is also, in part, a third-party coverage.

EXCLUSIONS

As with all coverages, auto medical payments coverage is subject to a number of exclusions, several of which are similar to exclusions applicable to auto liability coverages, including injury:

- ◆ arising out of transporting passengers for hire;
- ◆ covered by workers compensation benefits; or,
- ◆ arising out of racing or speed contests.

Motorcycle Exclusion

This medical payments exclusion precludes coverage for any injury sustained while occupying a motorized vehicle having less than four wheels. Technically, this exclusion would therefore also apply to other motor vehicles with less than four wheels, if such vehicles come within a given policy's definition of motor vehicle. Potentially, this could include snowmobiles and scooters that have become popular in recent years.

This is a provision in which insurers' policies often vary. Because of this potential variation, you should check to see what your policy does or does not cover if you have such an exposure. Nonetheless, if you own motorcycles or other such vehicles, a policy that is specifically applicable to such vehicles should apply first.

Public or Livery Conveyance Exclusion

This medical payments exclusion precludes coverage for bodily injury to an insured arising out of the transport of goods or persons for hire, with the exception of shared expense carpools. The reasons for this exclusion are the same as discussed with respect to the similar auto liability coverage exclusion. Persons engaged in such businesses need to purchase appropriate commercial policies.

Use of Vehicle as Residence or Premises Exclusion

This medical payments exclusion precludes coverage for bodily injury to an insured sustained while occupying any vehicle located for use as a residence or premises. The intent of this exclusion is to apply, for example, when a motor home or trailer is being used as a primary residence or an office or business premises. When the primary or exclusive use of such a vehicle is as a residence or premises, it is more properly the subject of a variant of homeowners policy whose medical payments coverage should apply in such circumstances.

This is again an example of an exclusion intended to avoid duplicative and overlapping coverage when another type of policy is intended to apply to the particular kind of risk presented.

Workers Compensation Exclusion

This auto medical payments exclusion precludes coverage for bodily injury to an insured occurring in the course of employment if workers compensation benefits are required to be provided or are available to cover that bodily injury in question.

An issue that may arise is whether the workers compensation exclusion precludes coverage when the injured party has not sought or received workers compensation benefits. The view of most states' courts is that the entitlement to workers compensation benefits is the controlling question, and the exclusion applies even if workers compensation benefits were neither sought nor received by the injured person.

Unrated Vehicles Exclusion

The definition of *your covered vehicle* encompasses not only the rated and described vehicles in the declarations, but also rented and borrowed vehicles. Your covered vehicle does not include owned vehicles that are not rated (described), newly acquired vehicles, or nonowned vehicles that are furnished to or regularly available for the use of an insured. This exclusion precludes medical payments coverage arising out of the latter categories of vehicles.

Family Member Owned Vehicles Exclusion

This exclusion is, in effect, an exception to the previous exclusion with respect to bodily injury sustained by an insured while occupying or struck by a vehicle other than your covered vehicle that is owned by, furnished to, or regularly available to a family member. This provision is commonly included in policies of insurers that do not use the ISO policy form.

This exclusion does not apply to the named insured or his or her spouse. This means that, if a family member owns or uses a vehicle that is not covered under the policy and the named insured or his or her spouse is injured while occupying or struck by such a vehicle, medical payments coverage will exist.

Nonpermissive Use Exclusion

This exclusion precludes medical payments coverage for bodily injury to an insured sustained while occupying a vehicle without a reasonable belief that the insured is entitled to do so. The goal of this exclusion is to defeat medical expense claims in circumstances where no reasonable person should expect insurance to apply. This exclusion's applicability will be highly dependent on the facts of a given claim, but some examples can illustrate the intent of this exclusion.

EXAMPLE 1: Your son steals a car and is injured while using it. No coverage would apply.

EXAMPLE 2: Your son or daughter is in a stolen car operated by one of their acquaintances and is injured. No coverage would apply.

In both cases, the injuries arise out of nonpermissive use of motor vehicles. Insurers exclude coverage for certain kinds of losses in order to create a deterrent to certain kinds of conduct that are likely to lead to loss. Common human experience teaches that in circumstances such as the previous examples, efforts to flee the scene of the crime or to escape the pursuit of law enforcement authorities are likely to result in accidents.

EXAMPLE: You forbid your child, another resident relative, or even your spouse from using a particular owned vehicle—the reason does not matter. Yet the prohibited person uses the vehicle or lets another person use it, and is injured. No medical payments coverage would apply in this circumstance.

The purpose behind this exclusion is to encourage responsible entrustment of vehicles and to avoid providing insurance coverage for persons who are perpetrators or participants in illegal or criminal activities.

Business Exclusion

Given the dual purposes of the average insured's use of vehicles, this exclusion is actually fairly limited in its scope. Recall, *business* is broadly defined as any trade, profession, or occupation. The medical payments business exclusion precludes coverage for bodily injury to an insured while occupying a vehicle when it is used in the business of an insured. The exclusion, however, contains an exception for injuries sustained while the insured is occupying:

- ◆ a private passenger auto;
- ◆ an owned pickup or van; or,
- ◆ a tractor attached to either category of vehicles.

If the injury arises out of occupying a private passenger auto, in an insured's business, the exclusion does not apply. Nor does the exclusion apply to injuries sustained while occupying owned pickups or vans used in an insured's business.

Well, what's left?—occupying a vehicle not owned by an insured, and used in the insured's business? This exclusion applies to injuries sustained while an insured is occupying nonowned vehicles other than private passenger autos (pickups, vans, or other vehicles), while such vehicles are being used in the insured's business. This means rented, borrowed, or employer-owned, nonprivate-passenger vehicles used in an insured's business.

War Exclusions

Insurance policies are intended to cover risks of loss arising from the normal incidents of life. The nuclear war, civil war, insurrection, rebellion, or revolution exclusions have long been held to be essentially uninsurable.

Governmental Coverage Exclusion

This exclusion appears in the ISO personal auto policy sold in some, but not all, states. This exclusion precludes automobile medical payments coverage for bodily injury to an insured who normally receives services or benefits for bodily injury from any agency, hospital, or other facility operated by any military or government. There is an exception if the person is legally required to pay for such services.

An exclusion of this nature has some pretty obvious purposes. The most apparent one is that of avoiding a double recovery by an insured who is entitled to free medical care as part of the conditions of his or her employment. A second, less obvious, purpose relates back to the *reasonable expenses* term used in the auto medical payments insuring agreement. Aside from what may or may not constitute reasonable expenses from the standpoint of a health maintenance organization or a managed care plan, what may or may not be a reasonable expense incurred in a military or governmental hospital or health-care facility may be so afflicted with proof problems that determining whether the cost, care, or services provided are *reasonable* can be impossible.

Finally, when services are provided to an insured by a government entity as part of that individual's employment, it is simply improper for other policyholders of that insurer to foot the bill through their insurance premiums when they are already footing the bill for those medical services as taxpayers.

Racing Competition Exclusion

The ISO personal auto policy auto medical payments coverage excludes bodily injury losses while an insured is occupying any vehicle located in a facility designed for racing.

This exclusion, when read fairly, is pretty limited. It applies only to bodily injury incurred within facilities designed for racing. It should come as a surprise to no one that racing and practicing for competition, would be excluded from coverage under an ordinary personal automobile policy. What needs to be understood, however, is that auto medical payments coverage terminates for anyone occupying the vehicle while it is located within a facility designed for racing.

EXAMPLE: An insured drives into the facility in a covered personal vehicle towing the trailer holding the racing vehicle and collides with another similar vehicle. An insured occupying the insured's personal vehicle injured in that collision would not be entitled to auto medical expense coverage. That does not mean, however, that the policy's auto liability coverage would not apply.

AUTO MEDICAL PAYMENTS LIMITS OF LIABILITY

There is fairly wide variation from one insurer to the next in regards to auto medical payments limits of liability. For example, the auto medical payments limit of liability provision of the ISO personal automobile policy addresses:

- ◆ the maximum limit of liability per accident;
- ◆ the interaction between the automobile medical payments coverage, the automobile liability coverage, and the uninsured and underinsured motorist coverage; and,
- ◆ the interaction between the auto medical payments limits of liability and the applicable limits of liability of coverages under other policies.

The first of these three provisions states that the limits of liability for the auto medical payments coverage in the policy's declarations is the maximum limit of liability for *each person in any one accident,* regardless of the number of insureds, claims made, vehicles involved, or premiums shown in the declarations. The auto medical payments limits apply on a per-person/per-accident basis.

EXAMPLE: A policy has a $5,000 auto medical payment limit of liability. When a couple is involved in an accident in which both are injured, they would be entitled to recover up to $10,000 (*i.e.*, up to $5,000 each). Limitations are discussed in the following paragraphs.

The second of these three provisions states that no one will be entitled to duplicate payments under the auto medical payments coverage for the same elements of loss for which that person recovers under the auto liability, uninsured, or underinsured motorist coverage. This is an example of a policy provision that reflects that coverage under insurance policies is intended to compensate an insured for injury (*i.e.,* to make the insured whole), not to provide an opportunity for profit by way of multiple recoveries.

The third of the auto medical payments limit of liability provisions is the *other insurance* clause. This provision states that if there is other applicable auto medical payments coverage, the insurer will pay only its share of the loss in the proportion that its auto medical payments limit of liability bears to the total applicable limits of all policies. This provision further states that the auto medical payments coverage applicable to any vehicle not owned by the insured will be applicable over any other auto medical payments insurance collectable by the insured. This latter provision reflects the general principle that the coverage of a policy as to a specifically described and rated vehicle applies as primary coverage. Where that circumstance does not exist, the coverage will apply only on an excess basis.

Some policies contain provisions intended to define *reasonable* medical expenses for purposes of the auto medical payments coverage. Their definitions use such terms as *reasonable charges for medical, surgical, X-ray, dental,*

ambulance, hospital, professional nursing, prosthetic devices, and funeral services.
Some insurers' policies further provide that medical expenses other than
funeral expenses will be reduced by:

- ◆ amounts payable under a workers compensation law or similar law;
- ◆ any amounts received from others, including their insurers, who
  may be legally responsible for the injuries; and,
- ◆ amounts of any other similar auto medical payments benefits
  payable to the injured person.

Some insurers' policies also include provisions in the nature of an exclusion for unreasonable or unnecessary medical expenses. Unreasonable medical
expenses are defined in terms of fees for medical services that are substantially
higher than the usual and customary charges for those services. Unnecessary
medical expenses are defined in terms of fees for medical services that are not
usually and customarily performed for treatment of the injury, including fees
for an excessive number, amount or duration of medical services.

These provisions are not exclusions per se, because the provisions do not
state that unreasonable or unnecessary medical expenses are not covered, but
rather, that the insurer reserves the right to contest such charges and to refuse
to pay them. These provisions further state that the insurer will defend the
insured if the insured is sued by a medical service provider because the
insurer has refused to pay contested medical expenses and will pay any resulting judgment. These provisions state that the insurer will select defense
counsel, establish the same duties of cooperation on the part of the insured as
applied under the personal liability coverage, and establish coverage for the
same categories of *Supplementary Payments* as apply to the liability coverage.

These latter provisions are intended to address the problem of excessive
and unnecessary medical expenses. They also put the burden of proof of rea-
sonableness and necessity on the medical service provider, while not leaving
the insured caught without coverage between the insurer's and medical service provider's respective positions. This is shown by the promise to defend the
insured and to pay any resulting judgment in a suit to collect fees for med-

ical services. This latter provision means that the medical service provider's bills will be paid if that service provider can, in fact, prove that the services rendered were reasonable and necessary.

Provisions of this nature seek to reduce claims costs without prejudice to the insured. When claims costs are held in check, premiums for all policyholders can be kept from escalating.

Chapter 17
Uninsured & Underinsured Motorist Coverage

Uninsured motorist and *underinsured motorist coverages* are intended to provide the insured with bodily injury coverage for losses that the insured is legally entitled to recover from the owner or operator of an uninsured or underinsured motor vehicle caused by an accident. In many states, uninsured motorist coverage is mandatory and the provisions of uninsured motorist policy provisions are commonly mandated by statute. In such states, insurers can issue policies with broader uninsured motorist coverage provisions and higher limits of liability than those mandated by law, but cannot issue policies with more restrictive provisions or with lower limits of liability.

COVERAGE

Uninsured motorist and underinsured motorist coverage applies to bodily injury to insureds as the result of accidents for which an uninsured or underinsured vehicle owner or operator is legally liable, but cannot pay because he or she is uninsured or underinsured. You might wonder why uninsured motorist and underinsured motorist coverage does not apply to property damage claims, other than as to the amount of the insured's collision damage deductible. This is because most persons purchase first-party auto physical damage coverage. When an insured third party is liable for property damage, that driver's liability insurance will cover property damage caused by that driver's negligent operation of the vehicle in question.

When the responsible driver is uninsured or underinsured, the property damage claim is still going to be a first-party claim, just covered under the first-party collision coverage. If you do not carry collision coverage on older vehicles because the costs of repair may well exceed the vehicle's value and you get involved in a collision with an uninsured or underinsured driver, you will be stuck for the damage to or loss of your car.

There are a couple of points that need to be made here. The advice to drop first-party collision damage coverage on any vehicle that still has significant utility is questionable. The purchase prices of vehicles, both new and pre-owned, continue to rise; so do the overall quality and useful lives of vehicles. While, in the event of a serious collision, repair costs may exceed a vehicle's value from a claims settlement standpoint, that does not mean that you will not be entitled to payment if your insurer determines your vehicle to be a total loss—you will receive an actual cash value payment.

Moreover, most uninsured motorist and underinsured motorist coverage include, or permit at a nominal charge, a collision deductible waiver with respect to the property damage caused by an accident with an uninsured or underinsured driver. If your older, but still useful, car or truck is damaged in a collision with an underinsured or uninsured motorist, the combination of your insurer's loss payment under your first-party collision coverage and the money from the uninsured motorist or underinsured motorist collision deductible waiver coverage can result in a significant recovery. Enough, at least, to contribute to the cost of a down payment on a replacement vehicle. You say, *Fine, but I'm still stuck with the costs of paying for a replacement vehicle. Why should I pay good money for collision coverage and for the collision deductible waiver applicable to uninsured and underinsured motorist coverage?*

The simple answer is that it is cheap and worth it. The premiums for collision coverage drop with the vehicle's age and degree of use (for example, odometer reading). And the premium for the uninsured motorist and underinsured motorist collision deductible waiver is usually less than a couple of dollars a month.

In short, uninsured motorist and underinsured motorist coverage is, relatively speaking, cheap for what you may recover. It serves a valuable societal purpose, because the funds that insureds can recover under uninsured motorist or underinsured motorist coverage reduce the sums that these persons may need to seek from various forms of public assistance.

DEFINITIONS

There are some relatively common features of uninsured motorist and underinsured motorist coverages. However, these coverages can vary widely from state to state, so you will need to seek information specific to your particular state from your agent or your state's department of insurance.

Uninsured motorist and underinsured motorist coverages are fairly complex. Unlike your comprehensive or collision coverage, you do not just simply report a claim, have your vehicle inspected by a claim adjuster, get repair estimates, and receive a check.

In order to better understand these coverages, you need to review the definitions of uninsured and underinsured vehicles. These are lengthy definitions, which will require some explaining. The ISO personal automobile policy definition of uninsured motor vehicle states:

> *"Uninsured motor vehicle" means a land motor vehicle or trailer of any type:*
>
> 1. *To which no bodily injury liability bond or policy applies at the time of the accident.*
>
> 2. *To which a bodily injury bond or policy applies at the time of the accident. In this case its limit for bodily injury liability must be less than the minimum limit for bodily injury liability specified by the financial responsibility law of the state in which "your covered auto" is principally garaged.*

> 3. *Which is a hit-and-run vehicle whose operator or owner cannot be identified and which hits:*
>   a) *You or any "family member";*
>   b) *A vehicle which your or any "family member" are "occupying"; or*
>   c) *"Your covered auto".*
> 4. *To which a bodily injury liability bond or policy applies at the time of the accident but the bonding insurance company:*
>   a) *Denies coverage; or*
>   b) *Is or becomes insolvent.*

However, *uninsured motor vehicle* does not include any vehicle or equipment:

> 1. *Owned by or furnished or available for the regular use of you or any "family member."*
> 2. *Owned or operated by a self-insurer under any applicable motor vehicle law, except a self-insurer which is or becomes insolvent.*
> 3. *Owned by any governmental unit or agency.*
> 4. *Operated on rails or crawler treads.*
> 5. *Designed mainly for use off public roads while not on public roads.*
> 6. *While located for use as a residence or premises.*

An underinsured motor vehicle is defined as follows:

> *"Underinsured motor vehicle" means a land motor vehicle for trailer of any type to which bodily injury liability bond or policy applies at the time of the accident but its limit for bodily injury liability is less than the limit of liability for this coverage.*

However, *underinsured motor vehicle* does not include any vehicle or equipment:

> 1. *To which a bodily injury liability bond or policy applies at the time of the accident but its limits to bodily injury liability is less than the minimum limit for bodily injury liabilities specified by*

the financial responsibility law of the state in which "your covered auto" is principally garaged.

2. *Owned by or furnished or available for the regular use of you or any "family member."*

3. *Owned by any governmental unit or agency.*

4. *Operated on rails or crawler treads.*

5. *Designed mainly for use off public roads while not upon public roads.*

6. *While located for use as a residence or premises.*

7. *Owned or operated by a person qualifying as a self-insurer under any applicable motor vehicle law.*

8. *To which a bodily injury liability bond or policy applies at the time of the accident but the bonding or insurance company:*

    a) Denies coverage; or

    b) Is or becomes insolvent.

The other significant uninsured motorist and underinsured motorist coverage definition is that of who qualifies as an insured for these coverages. The definition of *insured* in the ISO personal automobile policy uninsured motorist coverage extends to the named insured and any family member, any other person occupying your covered auto, and any person to which the uninsured motorist coverage applies that is entitled to recover damages because of bodily injury sustained by a person in the first two categories.

This third category's meaning is more than a little bit opaque. What it means in practical terms is that a spouse's loss of consortium claim arising from injury to the other spouse is covered under the uninsured motorist coverage if the spouse's injury is covered.

The definition of *insured* in the ISO underinsured motorist coverage endorsement is essentially the same as that applicable to the uninsured motorist coverage.

There are some common and important parallels between and concepts inherent in these definitions. First, and most obvious, is the concept of uninsured and underinsured. Uninsured is actually more complex, because, as the definition shows, it includes the notion of *phantom* vehicles—vehicles that are insured but for which the insurer denies coverage, and vehicles that are insured by insurers that become insolvent and unable to pay claims.

These provisions are intended to protect the insured from *genuine* uninsured and underinsured motorist loss exposures, not loss exposures for which there should be no reasonable expectation of coverage (*i.e.,* owned vehicles or otherwise available but uninsured vehicles). This includes vehicles owned by governmental agencies. (There are separate procedures in place for claims against governmental agencies.)

EXCLUSIONS

As stated before, the uninsured motorist and underinsured motorist coverages are complex. They are first-party coverages, and as such, the exclusions are important to understand. One of the most important exclusions is that these coverages do not apply to bodily injury sustained by an insured if the insured or his or her legal representative settles a bodily injury claim against the responsible third party without the insurer's consent. This provision is intended to avoid collusion between an uninsured or underinsured driver and the injured party as to the amount of the loss. The amount of the loss is something that should have a reasonably objective value. This provision prevents the insured and the uninsured motorist or underinsured motorist responsible from *setting up* the insurer when there has been no independent fact finder (*i.e.,* a judge or a jury) reaching a decision as to the amount of loss after hearing evidence.

Not surprisingly, the uninsured motorist and underinsured motorist coverages also exclude coverage for sums the insured is entitled to recover under workers compensation, disability, or other such laws. Nor do uninsured motorist and underinsured motorist coverages apply to punitive damages liability. Nor is there any coverage for bodily injury arising out of commercial uses of autos, such as the transportation of persons or cargo for hire.

Under uninsured motorist and underinsured motorist coverage, the insurer is entitled to a complete credit for any sums recoverable from:

- the responsible party;
- workers compensation or any other similar coverage;
- any personal injury protection coverage; or,
- any automobile medical payments coverage.

In other words, uninsured motorist and underinsured motorist coverage is *last dollar*, not *first dollar* coverage.

ARBITRATION

Finally, uninsured motorist and underinsured motorist coverages are made subject to mandatory arbitration clauses. This is one of the most important and complex parts of uninsured motorist and underinsured motorist coverages. If the insurer and the insured do not agree as to whether the insured is legally entitled to recover damages or the amount of loss, the dispute is subject to arbitration.

On a certain level, there is nothing about the arbitration provisions that should be a cause of concern to most policyholders. However, what you need to be aware of is that these mandatory arbitration provisions provide that each side is required to bear its own costs of the arbitration, including witnesses and an equal share in the cost of the arbitrator. This means that in an uninsured motorist or underinsured motorist arbitration, the policyholder must bear the expenses of expert witnesses as to causation of the accident (*i.e.,* the liability of the other driver) and damages. These expert witness costs can be significant.

LIMIT OF LIABILITY PROVISIONS

The uninsured motorist coverage provisions of the ISO personal automobile policy has its own separate limit of liability provision which states:

> *LIMIT OF LIABILITY*
>
> A. *The limit of liability shown in the Declarations for this coverage is our maximum limit of liability for all damages resulting from any one accident. This is the most we will pay regardless of the number of:*

1. *"Insureds";*
2. *Claims made;*
3. *Vehicles or premiums shown in the Declarations; or*
4. *Vehicles involved in the accident.*

The limit of liability provision of the ISO underinsured motorist coverage endorsement is essentially identical. The policies of insurers that do not use the ISO policy often add some different and additional provisions. These can include provisions that subject loss of consortium claims to your state's minimum financial responsibility laws' requirements and provisions that provide for offsets for workers compensation benefits received by the injured person.

OTHER UNDERINSURED MOTORIST COVERAGE PROVISIONS

The ISO underinsured motorist endorsement requires that a person seeking underinsured motorist coverage must promptly send the insurer copies of legal papers if a suit is brought by the insured. The insured must also notify the insurer in writing of a tentative settlement between the insured and the insurer of the underinsured motor vehicle. The insurer must be allowed thirty days to advance payment to that insured in an amount equal to the tentative settlement to preserve the insurer's rights against the other insurer, owner, or operator of such underinsured motor vehicle. This latter provision is intended to protect your insurer's subrogation rights against the responsible party or the insurer of the responsible party. A typical settlement includes a release of liability. Such a release would impair your insurer's subrogation rights.

The underinsured motorist coverage endorsement of the ISO policy also contains some additional provisions that amend the general subrogation clause of the ISO personal automobile policies general conditions. This provision further states that if the insurer advances payment, that payment will be separate from any amount the insured is entitled to recover under the provisions of the underinsured motorist coverage. The insurer also has the right to recover the advanced payment.

Chapter 18

Physical Loss or Damage Coverage Provisions

The physical loss or damage provision of personal auto policies are the principal first-party coverages afforded other than the uninsured motorist and underinsured motorist coverages. There are two main categories of covered physical damage losses:

◆ collision damage losses and
◆ losses other than collision.

Many people are probably at least a little bit familiar with these two categories, which are often referred to as *collision* and *comprehensive*. (The current ISO personal auto policy no longer uses the term *comprehensive* as the label for the category of covered physical damage losses that are not collision losses.)

The auto physical damage coverages of personal auto policies have relatively broadly worded insuring agreements and the boundaries of coverage are set largely by the exclusions. The insuring agreement of the ISO personal auto policy provides that the insurer will pay for direct and accidental loss to your covered auto or any nonowned auto, but only for loss caused by collision if the policy's declarations show that collision coverage is provided for that auto. For loss other than collision, the insurer will pay only if the declarations show that coverage for noncollision loss applies to that auto.

The insuring agreement then defines collision as, *the upset of your covered auto or a nonowned auto or their impact with another vehicle or object.*

The insuring agreement further proceeds to list ten categories of named perils that constitute covered physical damage losses other than collision. These ten categories of covered perils are:

1. missiles or falling objects;
2. fire;
3. theft or larceny;
4. explosion or earthquake;
5. windstorm;
6. hail, water, or flood;
7. malicious mischief or vandalism;
8. riot or civil commotion;
9. contact with bird or animal; and,
10. breakage of glass.

The manner in which the ISO personal auto policy is drafted leaves it somewhat unclear whether these ten categories are the only noncollision covered perils, or if these ten categories of perils (plus others that may occur) will be considered as other than collision losses. Reference to other insurers' policies suggests that ISO's intent was to provide all-risk coverage. In other words, the list of perils covered is intended to be nonexclusive. Coverage for a noncollision physical damage loss is included unless specifically excluded.

The ISO personal automobile policy's physical damage insuring agreement proceeds next to include a definition of *nonowned auto.* This includes private passenger autos, pickups, vans, or trailers not owned by, furnished, or available for the regular use of the named insured or any family member while in the custody of or being operated by, the named insured or any family member. It also includes any auto or trailer the named insured does not own while being used as a temporary substitute vehicle for the insured's covered auto that is out of normal use because of its breakdown, repair, servicing, loss, or destruction.

ADDITIONAL COVERAGES

Most personal auto policies include some additional coverages. The policies do not actually use this term; however, the concept fits. This is also an area where there is some variation between the policies offered by different insurers. Understanding the scope of these additional or supplementary coverages might be a reason for you to choose a policy from one insurer or another.

The ISO personal auto policy labels this category of coverages as *Transportation Expenses.* The ISO personal auto policy provides for payment of up to $15 per day, subject to a maximum of $450, for temporary transportation expenses actually incurred by the insured in the event of a loss to your covered auto. This coverage applies only if there is coverage for the underlying loss (*i.e.,* the policy covers comprehensive or collision losses). Higher daily limits and higher per-loss maximum limits are available from most insurers for nominal additional premiums. You merely need to ask what limits your insurer offers, learn how much the insurer charges, and make your own decision.

This coverage is not coverage for transportation expenses incurred because of breakdown of your vehicle. It applies only in the event of a covered collision or comprehensive loss and if you have paid an additional premium for the transportation expense coverage.

Under the ISO personal automobile policy, there are some limitations of which you should be aware. If loss is due to a *total theft* of your covered auto or of a nonowned auto, transportation expenses are payable during the period beginning forty-eight hours after the theft and ending when your auto is returned to you or the insurer pays for the loss.

If loss is due to a cause other than theft, coverage for transportation expenses applies only after your auto has been out of service for more than twenty-four hours. It is also limited to the amount of time reasonably required to repair or replace your car.

While the basic ISO personal auto policy does not include coverage for towing expenses, many auto insurers include coverage for towing your vehicle to a repair shop if it is disabled as the result of one of the comprehensive perils. There are commonly two preconditions for such towing coverage to apply: first, the insured must have purchased comprehensive coverage, and second, the work or labor must be performed on your vehicle at the place of its disablement.

Some insurers offer towing coverage subject to a specific dollar limit. Others reimburse for reasonable expense, recognizing that vehicles can become disabled as a result of covered causes of loss in inconvenient locations.

EXCLUSIONS

The first auto physical damage exclusion of the ISO personal auto policy is for loss that occurs while a covered vehicle is being used as a public or livery conveyance. As with the liability coverages of auto policies, this exclusion does not apply to loss occurring while the vehicle is being used in a shared-expense car pool.

The second auto physical damage exclusion applies to damage due and limited to wear and tear, freezing, mechanical or electrical breakdown or failure, or road damage to tires. This exclusion contains an exception if the damage results from a total theft of an insured vehicle.

This exclusion has parallels to the wear and tear, deterioration, and other property exclusions of homeowners policies. It is intended to reinforce the notion that insurance policies cover fortuitous losses, not losses that are inevitable (wear and tear) or the product of a failure to maintain (mechanical or electrical breakdown). However, if a mechanical breakdown occurs that results in collision, this exclusion would not apply to the resulting collision damage.

The third exclusion is actually six exclusions that combine the nuclear, war risk, and civil commotion exclusions.

The fourth auto physical damage exclusion is that applicable to electronic equipment such as stereo systems, CB radios, telephones, scanners, televisions, VCRs, personal computers, and accessories for such equipment.

This exclusion contains an exception for permanently installed equipment designed to be operated solely by the car's electrical system and equipment designed to be removed from its permanently installed housing in your auto (*i.e.,* removable face-plate car stereos).

The fifth auto physical damage exclusion precludes coverage for a total loss to a covered vehicle due to destruction or confiscation by governmental or civil authorities. This exclusion has an exception. It does not preclude coverage for the interests of a loss payee (*i.e.,* auto lender or lease company) in the covered auto. The purpose of this exception is to avoid inflicting the consequences of an insured's misconduct that results in governmental confiscation of a covered auto on the lender or lessor (which did not commit any misconduct).

The sixth exclusion precludes coverage for loss to a camper body or a trailer that you own that is not shown in the policy's declarations. There is an exemption for newly acquired campers or trailers if the insured reports the acquisition to the insurer and requests coverage within thirty days after acquiring ownership.

The seventh exclusion precludes coverage for loss for any nonowned auto when used by the named insured or a family member without a reasonable belief that the person in question is entitled to do so. In other words, you cannot use someone else's vehicle without permission and expect to be covered for damage to it.

The eighth exclusion precludes coverage for loss to awnings or cabanas, or equipment designed to create additional living facilities.

The ninth auto physical damage exclusion precludes coverage for loss to equipment designed to detect radar or laser. The intent of this exclusion is to deter use of radar and laser speed detection equipment. The underlying rationale for this exclusion is that people who use such equipment do so for the purpose of violating speed limits.

The tenth auto physical damage exclusion precludes coverage for loss to custom furnishings in pickups or vans. *Custom furnishings* or equipment are defined as including, but not limited to:

  ◆ special carpeting, insulation, furniture, or bars;
  ◆ facilities for cooking or sleeping;
  ◆ height extended roofs; or,
  ◆ custom murals, paintings, or other decals or graphics.

This exclusion has an intent similar to that of homeowners policy provisions that limit the amount of coverage for certain categories of property. Most insurers will allow the insured to *buy back* this exclusion, subject to full disclosure of the custom features included in a particular vehicle and payment of an appropriate additional premium.

The eleventh auto physical damage exclusion precludes coverage for nonowned autos used by any person while employed or engaged in the business of selling, repairing, servicing, storing, or parking vehicles. In other words, persons engaged in such businesses need to purchase the form of commercial auto policy appropriate to the particular type of auto-related business to cover such loss exposures.

The twelfth auto physical damage exclusion precludes coverage for loss to nonowned autos used by a person while employed or otherwise engaged in any business not listed in the prior exclusion. This exclusion has an exception for the maintenance or use by the named insured or family members of nonowned autos that are private passenger autos or trailers.

EXAMPLE 1: You are employed as a plumber and your employer gives you use of a company truck equipped with tools, equipment, and parts for use in the business and you are involved in a collision while in the course of your employment. The auto physical damage coverage of your policy would not apply to the damage to the truck.

EXAMPLE 2: You are an outside sales representative and you get use of a company private passenger auto. You are involved in a collision while in the course of your employment. This exclusion would not apply in this case.

The thirteenth exclusion of the auto physical damage coverages precludes coverage for loss to covered vehicles while located within any facility designed for racing for the purpose of competing, practicing, or preparing for any prearranged or organized race or speed contest. Coverage terminates once your vehicle enters such a facility. This is simply a risk outside the intended scope of personal auto policies.

The fourteenth and final exclusion of the auto physical damage coverages precludes coverage for loss to, or loss of use of, nonowned autos rented by the named insured or a family member. This exclusion applies if the rental vehicle company is precluded from recovering such loss from the named insured or family member by the terms of the rental agreement.

CONDITIONS

The auto physical damage coverage of the ISO personal auto policy includes a *conditions* section, although it is not so labeled. Most of the concepts are substantially similar to the conditions applicable to the property coverages of homeowners policies.

Limit of Liability

The first of the three subparagraphs of this condition states that the insurer's limit of liability will be the lesser of the actual cash value of the stolen or damaged property, or the amount necessary to repair or replace the property with other property of like kind and quality.

The second subparagraph of the limit of liability provision states that an adjustment of depreciation and physical condition will be made in determining actual cash value in the event of a total loss.

The third subparagraph of the limit of liability provision states that if repair or replacement results in better than like kind and quality, the insurer will not pay for the amount of the betterment.

This provision seemingly prevents a conundrum in light of the prevailing concept of actual cash value as the amount a willing buyer is inclined to pay a willing seller for an item of property. Depending on your local climate, modern day cars and vehicles can have a substantial utility, even though—given all our societal fascination for new cars—their actual cash value may be very, very low. It is this fact that forms the basis for the conventional wisdom that at some point in a vehicle's life, it no longer makes economic sense to continue to pay premiums for comprehensive and collision coverage.

There is no one-size-fits-all answer to the question of when to stop paying premiums, but the means to figure it out for yourself are readily available. There are three pieces of information you need to determine when it no longer makes economic sense to carry comprehensive and collision coverage on a particular vehicle.

First, you need to get a reasonable estimate of the remaining useful life of the vehicle. A mechanic should be able to suggest the likely repair and maintenance costs you should expect to incur in that remaining useful life.

Second, you need to determine the reasonable actual cash value of the vehicle. There are a variety of sources for this information, including the *Kelly Blue Book*, the Edmonds.com website, and *Consumer Reports*. These services provide regionally-adjusted wholesale and retail values for used vehicles depending on both mileage and condition.

Third, look at the declarations page of your policy and see what the premium charge for comprehensive and collision coverage on the vehicle in question is. If your comprehensive and collision premiums are still low compared to the actual cash value of your vehicle, it probably makes sense for most people to continue to maintain comprehensive and collision coverage. If the actual cash value of your car is still large enough that in the case of a total loss, you would still need or want a claim settlement to use toward a down payment for a replacement vehicle, then it is not yet time to drop collision damage and comprehensive coverage.

Loss Payment

This condition gives the insurer the option to pay the loss in money or to repair or replace the damaged or stolen property. If stolen property is recovered, the insurer has the option to return the property at its expense to the named insured, or to the address shown on the policy. If the insurer chooses to return recovered stolen property, it will pay for any damage to the property resulting from the theft. Your insurer also has the option of keeping all or part of the property in exchange for the payment. Finally, this condition provides that if the insurer settles the claim by means of a monetary payment, the payment will include applicable sales tax for the damaged or stolen property.

This latter provision is eminently fair. The insurer is, in effect, buying a totaled vehicle from you. As a result, you are going to have to make a significant financial outlay for the purchase of a replacement vehicle and will have to pay sales tax (in most states) on the purchase price. If the actual cash value of your totaled vehicle is $8,000, at a rate of 8%, the sales tax is $640—not an insignificant sum. Inclusion of sales tax in the loss payment by your insurer serves to make you whole.

No Benefit to Bailee

This condition is similar to that of homeowners property coverages. It provides that the auto physical damage insurance will not directly or indirectly benefit any carrier or other bailee for hire.

This condition is intended to make sure that if a bailee is responsible for damage to your car, it (or its insurer) should pay for the loss. It is not very common for the average person to put his or her vehicle in the custody of a carrier. When most people move these days, even cross-country, they often drive to their new location.

However, custody of our vehicles is given to others (bailees) on a regular basis. If you turn over your keys to parking attendants who park or move your car, you have created a bailment. Similarly, when you turn over your keys at an automobile dealership or repair shop, you have created a bailment.

Other Source of Recovery

This condition is a variation on an other insurance clause. It is generally worded the same, except it uses the phrase *other source of recovery* rather than just *other insurance*. The general statement of the condition is that the insurer will pay its share of loss in the proportion to its total applicable limits. The exception is that nonowned autos will apply only for excess coverage over any other insurance company, as well as any other source of recovery for the loss.

Appraisal

Auto physical damage coverages contain a contractual appraisal condition that is essentially identical to that of the property coverages of homeowners policies. In essence, this is a contractual arbitration provision that either the insurer or the insured can invoke when there is a dispute over the amount of loss. As is the case with the appraisal provisions of homeowners policies, the appraisal process cannot decide coverage questions.

In the auto physical damage coverage context, valuation issues most often arise when the vehicle is a total loss. Insurers frequently consult with appraisal services and data banks that maintain vehicle valuation information. The consumer has a greater ability to determine whether the insurer's valuation is accurate by virtue of these various services.

Because the insured and insurer must split the costs of appraisal on a 50-50 basis, do two things before demanding appraisal. First, ask your insurer to give you a copy of the appraisal report on which it is relying for its offer to settle your claim. Look it over to make sure that the report is using sales prices for the exact make, model, and model year of your vehicle, and that the features, conditions, and mileage are the same or similar to those of your vehicle. Also check for the geographic area from which the appraisal report got its information. Vehicle values vary widely from region to region.

Second, use one of the online vehicle valuation services to learn the regionally adjusted wholesale and retail prices for your vehicle. Be honest when inputting data relative to mileage and the condition of your vehicle. If the figures you come up with are close to what your insurer is offering and there are no obvious errors in the insurer's appraisal report, consider accepting the insurer's offer, or seek a compromise. Also, find out what paying your own appraiser will cost you. With that information, you should be able to figure out whether the costs, risks, and inconveniences of appraisal are likely to be worthwhile.

Duties after an Accident or Loss

This is a group of four conditions that are substantially similar to the insured's duties after loss on the property damage coverage of homeowners policies. This group of conditions applies to all the auto coverages, not just the physical damage coverage.

The first subparagraph requires the insured to give the insurer prompt notice of loss, including details as to how, when, and where the accident or loss occurred. This includes providing the names and addresses of any injured persons and witnesses.

The second subparagraph provides that the insured must:

- cooperate in the investigation, settlement, or defense of any claim or suit;
- promptly send the insurer copies of any notices or legal papers with respect to the accident or loss;
- submit as often as the insurer reasonably requires to:
  - physical examinations by doctors selected by the insurer and at the insurer's expense and
  - examinations under oath;
- authorize the insurer to obtain medical reports and other pertinent records; and,
- submit a proof of loss if required by the insurer.

The third subparagraph of the insured's duties after accident or loss relates solely to the uninsured motorist and underinsured motorist coverages. If the accident involves a hit-and-run driver, the insured must promptly notify the police. The insured must also promptly send the insurer copies of legal papers if a suit is brought.

Since it is usually the insured who is suing the other driver in an uninsured motorist or underinsured motorist situation, the insured must provide his or her insurer with a copy of the complaint against the other driver as well as all other legal papers served by both parties in the suit. This is because one of the preconditions to recovery of uninsured motorist or underinsured motorist benefits by the insured is proof that the uninsured motorist or underinsured motorist is legally liable to the insured for damages.

The fourth and final paragraph of the insured's duties after accident or loss applies to the physical damage coverage. The insured must take reasonable steps after loss to protect a covered vehicle and its equipment from further loss. Such reasonable expenses will be reimbursed by the insurer. An example of reasonable steps might include having the vehicle towed to a repair shop where it can be secured pending examination by the insurer's adjusters.

The insured must promptly notify the police if a covered vehicle is stolen. The insured must permit the insurer to inspect and appraise damaged property before it is repaired or disposed of.

In this regard, just as is the case with property coverage of your homeowners policies, you should obtain written confirmation from your insurer that it is permissible to dispose of damaged property before you do so.

General Provisions

The final section of the ISO personal auto policy is titled, *General Provisions.* This is essentially another group of conditions, most of which are substantially similar to homeowners policy general conditions.

Bankruptcy

This condition states that the bankruptcy of the insured will not relieve the insurer of its obligations under the policy. This is a standard provision that appears in essentially all liability policies issued in the United States.

Changes

This condition addresses three separate issues. First, it states that the policy contains all of the agreements between the insurer and the insured, and that the terms of the policy may not be changed or waived except by way of an endorsement issued by the insurer.

The second concept included in the condition is the insurer's right to change the premium during the middle of the policy term if there is a change in the information on which the policy is based, including but not limited to:

- the number, type, or use of insured vehicles;
- the number of operators;
- the place where vehicles are garaged; or,
- changes in coverages afforded, deductibles, or limits of liability.

The third concept included in this condition states that if the insurer makes a change that broadens coverage under *this edition* of the policy without an additional premium, the change will apply automatically as of the date of the insurer's implementation of the change.

Fraud

This condition provides that coverage is negated for *any insured* who has made fraudulent statements or engaged in fraudulent conduct with respect to any accident or loss for which coverage is sought.

Legal Action Against Us

This is a standard policy provision. This condition first provides that no lawsuits can be brought against the insurer unless there has been full compliance with all the policy's terms. This provision cannot bar a person from suing his or her insurer. Rather, it provides the insurer with a defense to such a suit when there has been a material breach of policy terms, such as a refusal to submit to an examination under oath or failure to comply with proof of loss requirements.

The second portion of this condition states that no lawsuit may be brought against the insurer by a claimant against the insured, unless the insurer agrees in writing that the insured has a legal obligation to pay damages, or judgment has been enforced. Again, this provision cannot bar a claimant from filing a lawsuit against your insurer. Rather, this provision gives the insurer a defense to the lawsuit where these preconditions are not satisfied.

Finally, this condition states that no one can bring the insurer into a lawsuit in which the liability of the insured will be determined.

NOTE: *The law of a very limited number of states permits the insurer to be named the defendant along with the insured.*

Our Right to Recover Payment

This condition contains the personal auto policy's subrogation provisions. When an insurer makes a payment for a loss for which a third party is legally responsible, the insurer becomes subrogated (*i.e.,* succeeds) to the insured's rights to recover from that third party. This condition provides that the insured must cooperate with the insurer in enforcing its subrogation rights against the responsible third party and must do nothing to prejudice the insurer's subrogation rights, such as, for example, releasing the responsible party.

This condition also provides that if the insured recovers damages from the responsible party and the insurer has paid the claim, the insured must hold the recovery in trust for the insurer and reimburse the insurer to the extent of the claim payment.

Policy Period and Territory

This condition provides that the policy's coverage applies only to accidents and losses that occur during the policy period shown in the policy's declarations. It further provides that the policy territory is the United States, its territories and possessions, Puerto Rico, and Canada. (Coverage applies to loss or damage involving covered vehicle while being transported between the ports of the covered policy territories.)

For most persons, it is more important to recognize where coverage will not apply. First, coverage does not apply in Mexico. You need to purchase a separate policy if you wish to drive into and in Mexico. The policy must be purchased from an insurer licensed to issue policies in Mexico. There are significant differences between the laws of the United States and Mexico and in the absence of a policy with coverages that conform to Mexican law, you could face being jailed or having your vehicle impounded in the event of an accident. Under Mexican law, traffic accidents and property damage and bodily injury arising out of accidents are both criminal and civil matters.

Second, the *transport* coverage only applies between ports of covered territory—while on a ferry between Seattle and Vancouver, British Columbia, for example. If you buy a car for European delivery, your United States auto policy will not cover loss or damage occurring while the car is in shipment to the United States. Again, you need to purchase separate coverage for such an exposure.

Termination

This condition contains the policy's cancellation and nonrenewal provisions. Almost every state has statutory requirements, which are added to policies by means of endorsements that contain the state's limitations on the insurer's right to cancel or nonrenew a policy and the amount and kind of notice required for an effective notice of cancellation or nonrenewal.

The insured's failure to pay premiums is a permissible ground for cancellation. Also, if your driver's license has been suspended or revoked, or if any driver who lives with you or who customarily uses your covered auto is suspended or revoked, the insurer may cancel the policy. Finally, the insurer may terminate if it discovers that the policy was obtained through material misrepresentation.

The ISO personal auto policy also contains two automatic termination provisions. The first of these states that if the insurer has offered to renew or continue coverage and the insured fails to pay the premium, the policy will automatically terminate at the end of the current policy period.

The second provision states that if the insured obtains any other insurance on your covered auto, any similar insurance provided by the policy will terminate for that auto on the effective date of the other policy. Such provisions may conflict with your state's laws governing cancellation of policies and may not be enforceable.

Transfer of the Insured's Interest under the Policy

This is another standard American insurance policy condition. It provides that the named insured's rights under the policy cannot be assigned without the insurer's written consent. This provision reinforces the concept that insurance policies are personal contracts between the insured and the insurer. While items of property may be the subject of a policy and their physical characteristics are important, the contract is between the insured and the insurer. It is the insured's conduct and standing that matters to the insurer. Hence, assuming acceptability of a new and different insured to the insurer after the sale of a house or a car, the insurer may be willing to issue a policy to the new owner. But it is under no obligation to do so. And, the insured cannot circumvent the insurer's rights by assigning his or her rights under a policy.

In event of the death of the named insured, this condition does provide that the spouse of the named insured will be covered, as will be the estate's legal representative (*i.e.,* executor). Such coverage applies only until the end of the policy period. Depending on the length of time needed to close the estate or on the actual persons who will be driving the vehicle while the estate is open, the executor may need to obtain additional coverage. For example, if the title to the vehicles is held solely in the name of a deceased husband, the executor of the estate probably needs to obtain an auto policy in the name of the estate, the executor, and all persons who have use of the vehicles until the estate is settled.

Two or More Auto Policies

This is a policy condition that is pretty much exclusive to personal auto policies. It provides that if:

> *this policy and any other auto insurance policy issued to you by us apply to the same accident, the maximum limit of our liability under all the policies shall not exceed the highest applicable limit of liability under any one policy.*

This is intended to be merely an antistacking provision. If several policies issued by the same insurer to the same insured apply to the same loss, there is nothing inherently unfair about a contractual provision that states that only the highest applicable policy limit applies, not the limits of all applicable policies.

However, the very existence of this provision seemingly undermines the automatic termination provision previously discussed. This provision expressly contemplates the possibility that the insured might for various reasons obtain several policies, including from the same insurer, that could result in overlapping coverages. Under the rules of policy interpretation applicable in many states, the foregoing condition is yet another reason why the automatic termination clause may well be unenforceable, particularly under the facts of a specific situation.

Chapter 19

Life, Credit Life, Disability, and Health Coverage

This chapter sets out some overall concepts to assist you in deciding which types of life insurance, disability insurance, and health-care coverage may be of interest or necessity to you. No attempt to review these types of policies/contracts provision by provision as was done with homeowners and personal auto policies is made.

LIFE INSURANCE

There are numerous forms of life insurance—there are undoubtedly dozens, if not hundreds, of permutations of life insurance contracts. There are always specialized needs, and almost always there is an insurer willing to tailor a policy to meet a specific need.

The different types of policies include term life insurance, ordinary or whole life insurance, and the various permutations of the same, including adjustable, universal, and variable life policies. In addition, there are various forms of credit life policies. These are mostly examples of individually underwritten and owned policies.

There are also some kinds of life insurance policies that are more commonly marketed and sold on a group basis subject to a master policy. These can include some forms of credit life insurance, as well as accidental death coverages that are often marketed to persons who share some qualifying characteristic or membership. For example, many credit card issuers include such coverages automatically upon issuance of the credit card, or, upon purchase of an airline ticket with that credit card. Such coverages can be offered through memberships of organizations like the AARP, NRA, bar or medical associations, or even through commercial outlets.

For example, the *Los Angeles Times* has for decades offered to its subscribers the opportunity to participate in a low cost, group accidental death life insurance program. Available limits are relatively high and annual premiums are very low. Coverages are somewhat more restrictive than individually owned life insurance policies. Nonetheless, for younger persons whose primary exposure to fatality is some sort of accident and who may want or need higher life insurance limits than they could afford by means of term or whole life policies, such low-cost, group accidental death policies can be a useful adjunct to the coverages of individual life policies.

Term Life Insurance

Term life insurance, or level premium term life insurance, is *pure* life insurance. The premiums you pay purchase coverage for the policy limit specified in the limits of liability for the term of the policy. There is no cash value, dividend, or investment component to term life insurance. The premiums for term life insurance, whether paid annually, semiannually, quarterly, or monthly, remain fixed throughout the term of the policy. When the term of the policy ends, you must apply for and obtain a new policy if you wish to continue to maintain life insurance coverage.

The premiums charged for term life insurance policies depend on the following primary variables:

- ◆ the age of the person whose life is to be insured;
- ◆ whether that person is or is not a smoker;
- ◆ other significant health issues or conditions;
- ◆ the duration of the term for which coverage is sought; and,
- ◆ the policy limits applied for.

Premiums for term life insurance have been quite low in recent years, at least for nonsmokers without any other significant health issues. There is a great deal of competition among insurers for term life business, which means low cost coverage for the consumer.

Indeed, in the not too distant past, many term life policies were issued for five or ten year terms. After that term expired, the insured would have to purchase a replacement policy, but at the higher rates charged for the older age group of which the insured was then a member. In contrast, many term life insurers are now offering twenty and thirty year level premium term life policies, including to persons in their forties, at premiums only slightly higher than those charged for five and ten year term policies for younger age groups in the recent past.

A young nonsmoker in good health employed in a nonhazardous occupation should be able to purchase a $200,000 to $300,000 term life insurance policy for only a few hundred dollars annually. A middle-aged person with the same good health characteristics should be able to purchase a term life policy for only $500 to $700 annually. (You can assume premiums for policies with higher limits have larger premiums in proportion to the higher limits purchased.)

Many financial advisors advocate term life insurance as the only way to go. Their point of view is that the rates of return on the savings/cash value, dividend, or investment aspects of the various forms of whole life insurance are low compared with other investment vehicles. They believe that a person should only buy term life insurance and should invest the difference between the cost of term and whole life insurance in other more *fruitful* investment choices.

The primary disadvantages to term life insurance are that if you purchase relatively short-term policies (*i.e.,* five to ten years), you will have to pay more in premiums for a replacement policy because of your increased age, assuming all other underwriting factors remain unchanged. The latter point is the other disadvantage of term life insurance, particularly as the insured starts to advance in age. If you develop a serious, diagnosed health problem, you might not be able to obtain a replacement policy at all, or only at a highly increased premium. In contrast with the various forms of whole life coverage, the policy remains in force, at level premiums, from inception until you die, as long as you pay the premiums on time.

Whole Life Insurance

Whole, or ordinary, life insurance is a form of life insurance that provides life-time protection as long as the insured pays the premium. While there are some minor variations of this basic concept—such as single premium policies in which the entire premium is paid at the outset or policies under which the insured pays premiums for a stated period of years or until the insured reaches a certain age—most ordinary or whole life policies provide for payment of level premiums for the life of the insured and of the policy.

Premiums may be payable on an annual, semiannual, quarterly, or monthly basis. Many policyholders elect monthly payments due to the magnitude of whole life premiums—it makes budgeting easier. In order to accommodate budgeting, many insurers will set up automatic debits from their checking account so that they do not have to incur the inconvenience of writing and mailing a check each month.

Whole life policies have two primary components. A portion of the premium purchases the death benefit coverage throughout the insured's life. The other component of the premium goes to build up the cash value account. In the event of the insured's death, the beneficiary is paid the death benefit (*i.e.,* the policy limit) *plus* the accumulated cash value. The policy generally guarantees a fixed rate of return (*i.e.,* interest) on the funds in the cash value account. These rates are generally low and tend to be reasonably consistent with prevailing bank savings and certificate of deposit rates (although the accumulation of the cash value account is not subject to income tax, with some limited exceptions).

Under a standard whole life policy, the insured may be paid a cash dividend by the insurer depending on the insurer's financial performance. The dividend can be used by the insured to reduce or offset premiums due, to purchase higher limits of insurance, or to purchase term insurance.

The cash value development is one of the reasons many persons purchase whole life policies. The cash value account can be borrowed against without the necessity of qualifying for a law as would be the case with a bank or other lending institutions. In addition, should the insured choose to *surrender* the policy, the cash value account, plus accumulated interest, is paid to the insured. Sometimes retired persons who no longer have a need for the death benefit (for example, their mortgage is paid off and their children are done with college) will surrender a life policy and use the cash value account to purchase an annuity that provides an income stream.

The provisions governing loans from the cash value account of a whole life policy are part of the policy's terms and conditions. It is the *forced savings* aspects of whole life policies and the cash value accumulation that make them attractive to many persons. If there is an automatic monthly debit from your checking account or you are writing a check every month to keep the policy in force, it is harder to spend that money on something else. Notwithstanding the advice of some financial advisors to *buy term insurance and invest the difference*, not everyone is disciplined enough to do so.

The rates of return on the cash value accounts of whole life policies are generally lower than other potential investment vehicles. However, the cash value accounts of whole life policies are usually guaranteed and most states have life and health insurance guaranty funds, which provide some protection in the event of an insurer insolvency. Few other investment vehicles have such guaranties or safeguards. For example, while ordinary bank, savings and loan accounts, and certificates of deposit are insured by the FDIC, the limits of coverage are low. By contrast, the California life and health guarantee fund statutes provide the following recoverable limits in the event of a life insurer insolvency:

- ◆ $250,000 in life insurance death benefits per policy;
- ◆ $100,000 in net cash value withdrawal or surrender benefits per policy;
- ◆ $100,000 in present value of annuity benefits per annuity contract; and,
- ◆ $5,000,000 maximum per person where a person owns multiple policies and/or annuity contracts.

A point frequently overlooked by those who advocate *buy term and invest the difference* is the basic investment strategy of diversification. Yes, a whole life policy can be regarded as a low yield investment. It is, however, more secure than many alternatives. Most investment advisors would be hard-pressed to disagree with the proposition that a person's investments and savings need to be distributed among investment vehicles with higher, lower, and intermediate levels of risk. Viewed in this light, whole life coverage is something worthy of consideration—not as a person's sole investment, but as a component.

Whole Life Variations

Because of some of the criticisms of the low investment/savings yield characteristics of standard whole life policies, life insurers have developed variant forms of whole life coverage that have the potential to deliver somewhat higher investment yields. However, these come with greater degrees of investment risk. Common categories of such variant whole life products are adjustable life, universal life, and variable life policies.

Each of these types of policies provides a death benefit and is usually a level premium policy for the lifetime of the insured. They differ from conventional whole life policies in how the cash value account is handled.

Variable Life Policies

Variable life policies are the riskiest of these three categories. The cash value account is not guaranteed by the insurer. Depending on the insurer and the policy, the insured decides what investment vehicle the cash value portion of the premium will be invested in. The available investment options may be the same investment funds managed and operated by the insurer that its variable annuity customers can choose to invest their annuity balance in. These are like mutual funds in the sense that they involve different balances between stocks and bonds or other market sectors, but are usually not publicly traded.

Because of these aspects of variable life policies, the cash value account is subject to the general market conditions and the risk of decline in investment value, as well as gains. So, while variable life policies create the potential for greater cash value accumulation than standard whole life policies, they also include a risk of investment loss not presented by standard whole life policies. As a result, variable life policies can only be sold by persons who possess a *National Association of Securities Dealers* (NASD) license and who are registered with the *Securities and Exchange Commission*.

Universal Life Policies

This form of whole life insurance is much closer in concept to standard whole life insurance. Unlike a standard whole life policy, which has a fixed interest rate on the cash value account for the life of the policy, the universal life policy has a guaranteed minimum interest rate. This rate can fluctuate up in response to the insurer's financial performance and general market conditions.

Many life insurers permit a universal life policy to grow with the insured. They contain provisions that periodically permit the insured to increase the policy limit by a percent specified in the contract, without the requirement of proving insurability, at a commensurately larger premium. Such provisions usually also accelerate the rate of cash value build up. Often, such increases in limits provisions stipulate that once the insured refuses to accept a periodic increase in limits, the policy limit and premium then becomes fixed for the life of the policy. From that point forward, it cannot be increased further, except by cancellation and rewriting a new policy, subject to new proof of insurability.

Universal life policies also let the insured change the amount of the death benefit and the amount and timing of premium payments from time to time. Increases in the death benefit often require new proof of insurability. Universal life policies can be structured so that when dividends are paid by the insurer, they can be credited to the cash value account.

Adjustable Life Policies

Adjustable life policies are similar to universal life policies, and indeed, none of these categories is strictly defined. Insurers often offer policies that combine various features of adjustable, universal, and variable life policies. Almost any permutation is possible.

Adjustable life policies are more in the nature of hybrids between term and whole life policies. In addition to allowing the insured the option of periodically altering the death benefit level (with corresponding changes in premiums due), adjustable life policies also allow the insured the flexibility to switch the coverage to term coverage for a period (during which there will be no additions to the cash value account), and later to switch back to whole life.

This feature can be attractive to persons who anticipate occasional cash flow crunches. This type of policy could potentially be attractive to a self-employed person whose income might fluctuate or to persons who wish to get started on a whole life policy early in life, at an age when their rates will be lower, but who may wish the flexibility to switch temporarily to term coverage to reduce premiums. This can be due to a sudden blip in their budget, such as the birth of a child or saving for the down payment on a house or condominium, or various other reasons.

Choosing What Is Best for You

Most of the major personal lines property and casualty insurers also offer life products. No doubt you have seen their television commercials. However, many life insurance agents represent only one insurer, such as Prudential Life, MONY (Mutual of New York), Metropolitan Life, or Northwestern National Life.

Other agents may have the ability to place policies with multiple insurers. Term life insurance is one of the few forms of insurance coverage the average person might reasonably consider buying through the Internet. There are several websites that permit a person to obtain multiple quotes. If you have decided that term life insurance is all you want or need, then using one of those sites is just fine.

No life insurer will issue a policy without proof of insurability. All insurers require a signed application (to provide a basis for fraud defenses to coverage within the contestable period, for such rating factors as age, whether the insured is a smoker, health issues, etc.). The application includes detailed questions about your medical history. The application states that the insurer is relying on the representations in the application in making its decision whether to issue a policy to you and in determining the amount of premium to charge. The application normally is incorporated into the policy.

In addition, you must submit to a medical examination whose intent is to confirm whether your answers to certain of the questions on the application were truthful. Mostly, the medical examination consists of an appointment with a licensed venipuncturist (someone licensed under the laws of your state to draw blood specimens). At that appointment, the venipuncturist will typically ask for proof of identification, take a blood specimen, and will usually ask you a detailed list of questions about whether you are a smoker and many if not all of the same medical history questions as were on the application.

The blood specimen taken will reveal one's HIV status, whether you are infected with any of the hepatitis viruses or syphilis, or reveal liver function, which, in turn can divulge many things about the state of your health. It also will reveal cholesterol levels and blood sugar levels, as well as your use of drugs or steroids.

In the traditional life insurance policy sales transaction, the agent completes the application, has you sign it, takes your check for the premium or deposit for the premium, and the policy is issued effective the date of the application (subject to review and approval of the application and the results of the medical examination). If the results of your medical exam reveal a material difference between what you stated on the application, your application is usually evaluated and underwritten again. You will probably receive a counterproposal, often involving a higher premium than that originally quoted. In such a circumstance, the effective date of a life insurance policy will be the date the applicant accepts the insurer's counteroffer, usually by delivering payment of the difference between the deposit premium and the larger premium quoted in the counteroffer.

Insurable Interest

An insured may take out a life insurance policy on his or her own life for the benefit of named beneficiaries (which may include natural persons, or entities such as churches, schools, or any other organization) or for the benefit of his or her own estate. An insured has an insurable interest in his or her own life in providing a source of funds for his or her intended beneficiaries. But there are many other uses of life insurance policies. For example, where partners in a business have a buy/sell agreement in place in the death of either, each is most often the owner of the policy covering the life of the other. That means control over payment of premiums and keeping the policy in force remains in the hands of the person for whose benefit the policy was taken out in the first place.

When a person other than the insured is to be the owner of a life insurance policy, there is some interest or obligation—usually economic—that needs to be secured or protected by the policy in the event of the death of the person insured. The reason why policy ownership is placed in the hands of a person other than the insured is to prevent the insured from *meddling* with the policy. This meddling may include letting it lapse by nonpayment of premiums or by changing the beneficiary to defeat the economic obligation that the policy was procured to protect.

In order for such a policy to be enforceable in situations in which the insured and owner of the policy are different persons, there must be some basis for the owner to be able to show an *insurable interest* in the insured's life. This requires the existence of collateral documentation why a policy is being issued on the life of Person A where the policy is to be owned by Person B.

General Life Insurance Policy Provisions

While the specific provisions of life insurance policies will not be discussed, some general terms, common to life insurance policy provisions need to be highlighted. These are:

- ◆ the incontestability clause;
- ◆ the suicide exclusion;
- ◆ lapse; and,
- ◆ what happens upon the simultaneous death of the insured and the beneficiary.

Incontestability Clause

One of the necessary incidents of a life insurance policy is that after the insured has passed away, he or she cannot be questioned about his or her motives or representations made when applying for the policy. Problems arose when at times insurers investigated and contested claims under life insurance policies and attempted to avoid liability for payment or attempted to rescind policies after the death of the insured based on alleged fraud, concealment, or misrepresentation in procuring the policy. Eventually, disputes of this nature resulted in the inclusion in most life insurance policies of incontestability clauses.

Such clauses provide that after a period of time stated in the policy, usually two years, the insurer may not revoke the policy based on an alleged misrepresentation in the application. Two years is considered to be a reasonable time within which the insurer can complete any investigation of statements made by the insured in the application involving his or her insurability.

A sample incontestability clause states:

With respect to statements made in the application, this Policy is not contestable after it has been in force during the insured's lifetime for a period of two years beginning with the Date of Issue shown in the Schedule. With respect to statements made in an application for reinstatement, the Policy is not contestable after it has been in force during the insured's lifetime for a period of two years beginning with the date of reinstatement.

Suicide Clause

The issue of suicide has long been a problem for life insurers. These issues included moral and religious revulsion against suicide, let alone the prospect of a person intent on suicide taking out life insurance as a means of satisfying debts he or she otherwise could not. The current suicide clause in modern life insurance policies reflects a long history of disputed and litigated claims.

Common suicide clauses preclude coverage for death by suicide or severely restrict the benefits recoverable if a death by suicide occurs within the first two years after the policy's issuance. The current suicide clause is the product of research that indicates that the great majority of cases in which an insured has committed suicide in order to make life insurance proceeds available to a beneficiary or creditors have occurred within a short time after the policy has been taken out.

A current sample suicide clause states:

> *If the insured, while sane or insane, dies by suicide within two years of the Date of Issue shown in the Schedule, the death proceeds under this Policy will be an amount equal to the premiums paid less the loan balance as of the date of death.*

Generally, there is a presumption against suicide. Since the suicide clause is in the nature of a policy exclusion, the insurer would bear the burden of proof that the insured's death was the result of suicide. In many cases, the insured will make this burden of proof an easy one for the insurer to sustain, for example, by leaving a suicide note. You might be surprised, however, in how many cases the insurer cannot sustain its burden of proof based on the presumption against suicide.

Lapse and Reinstatement

Most life insurance policies contain provisions governing the effect of a failure to pay premiums, which usually results in lapse of the policy and procedures for reinstatement after lapse. These provisions are relatively generous.

Usually there is a thirty or thirty-one day grace period within which the insured can pay late premiums and avoid a lapse in coverage (a good reason to agree to a monthly automatic debit from your checking account). The policy remains in effect during the grace period. If the insured dies during the grace period, the amount of the unpaid, overdue premium will be deducted from the loss payment to the beneficiary.

When a policy is eligible for reinstatement (and the conditions will be stated in the policy), an insured may seek reinstatement by sending the insurer:

- ◆ proof of insurability;
- ◆ payment of all outstanding premiums plus interest at a percentage stated in the policy and compounded, usually annually; and,
- ◆ payment of any outstanding loan balance and interest thereon (this would not apply to term life policies that have no cash balance account).

There is usually a time limit on seeking reinstatement, which can range from one to five years. The insurer has the right to approve or disapprove the reinstatement application. The date of reinstatement, if approved, is usually the date the insured has complied with all the insurer's conditions precedent to reinstatement.

Simultaneous Death of Insured and Beneficiary

A recurring circumstance occurs when the insured and the beneficiary under a life insurance policy die as the result of the same accident or occurrence. The law of the majority of jurisdictions is that the insured is presumed to have survived the beneficiary. Thus, the policy proceeds will be paid to the contingent beneficiary of the insured (if there is one designated in the policy) or to the insured's estate if there is no contingent beneficiary.

A person seeking to contest this presumption has the burden of proving that the insured, in fact, predeceased the beneficiary. A person who might seek to raise such a challenge would usually be a person entitled to share in the estate of the beneficiary who is not entitled to share in the estate of the insured.

CREDIT LIFE INSURANCE

Credit life insurance is usually marketed on a direct mail basis by credit card issuers and mortgage lenders. The credit card issuers and mortgage lenders usually contract with an insurer to actually underwrite and issue coverage and do not usually act as the insurer. At a growing rate, the credit card issuers and mortgage lenders have established or acquired affiliates or subsidiaries through which they issue such coverage.

Credit life policies typically provide for payment of the outstanding credit card or mortgage balance in the event of the death of the insured. The premiums for credit life coverage vary with the amount of the covered outstanding indebtedness.

Credit life insurance is almost always a bad deal for the consumer. With credit life insurance the only person or entity that is going to receive any payment is the credit card issuer or mortgage lender. Instead, buy term life insurance that will provide your beneficiaries not only with funds to satisfy your outstanding debts, but also additional funds for their needs (assuming, of course, your term life limits cover all those needs).

DISABILITY INCOME INSURANCE

Disability insurance, also known as *disability income insurance*, is a form of health insurance that provides coverage to replace a portion of the insured's income if he or she becomes temporarily or permanently disabled as the result of sickness, accident, or injury.

Disability coverage can have a lot of variables. First, most disability policies have a waiting period (often referred to as an elimination period) after the disability commences before the insured can start collecting benefits. Common waiting periods are thirty, sixty, ninety, and 180 days. The longer the elimination period, the lower the premiums are.

Disability policies also vary in the period for which benefits are payable. These periods can range from as short as two years, to as long as until the insured reaches the age of 65, the *usual* age at which most persons retire. The longer the period of benefits coverage, the larger the premiums.

Disability policies also vary in the amount of benefits payable, usually expressed as a percent of the insured's predisability income. Generally, disability policies will limit benefits to no more than 60% of the insured's income. This limit is intended to account for the insured's loss of *net* income, not gross income. This is done because disability benefits are usually not taxable, and someone who is no longer receiving payment of wages is no longer paying Social Security and Medicare taxes. Further, disability policies often contain provisions requiring coordination of the benefits payable with other recoveries the insured may be receiving, such as Social Security disability payments, so that the insured is not receiving greater net income by way of disability benefits than he or she did before the disability occurred. These provisions are all intended to avoid providing an incentive for malingering.

Disability policies can also vary in their definitions of disability. There are usually separate definitions of *partial disability* and *total disability.* The definitions also vary in whether *disability* is defined in terms of the insured's disability to perform the duties of his or her occupation immediately prior to commencement of disability or the insured's disability to perform the duties of any gainful employment in an occupation that would provide income commensurate with that earned prior to disability.

Individual disability income policies are available and tend to be quite expensive. Much of the disability income coverage sold in the United States is provided through employer-sponsored or other group plans. For many persons, participation in such a group disability income plan, if available, may be the only realistically affordable way to obtain any such coverage. Even then, premiums can be fairly substantial, especially in light of the fact that many persons also need to contribute to health insurance premiums and pay for life, homeowners, and auto insurance.

Choosing a longer elimination period such as ninety or 180 days, can help lower premiums to the point where they are affordable. If you choose such a ninety or 180 day elimination period, you need to have enough savings to cover your income loss during that period, once your paid sick leave (if any) has been used up.

HEALTH INSURANCE POLICIES AND MANAGED CARE PLANS

There are two primary forms of private health-care coverage in the United States (this excludes Medicare and similar state law health-care systems for the indigent). There are health insurance policies and managed care plans. Managed care plans greatly predominate over health insurance policies. Indeed, the differences between health insurance policies and the various forms of managed care plans continue to diminish.

Both types of private health-care coverage are heavily regulated by the federal and state governments. Persons wishing to obtain a state-specific summary of their own state's laws regulating health-care policies and plans, which also include discussions of applicable federal statutes and regulations, should visit

www.healthinsuranceinfo.net. This is a website created and maintained by the Georgetown University Institute for Health Care Research and Policy.

It is not unreasonable at present to characterize health-care coverage as something that no longer constitutes *insurance* in the traditional sense. Most persons in the United States no longer have health insurance per se, but rather, are members of, or subscribe to, a service plan under which they receive health-care services from a health maintenance organization (HMO) or some other form of managed care plan. Traditional health indemnity policies, under which an insured paid his or her health-care provider, executed an assignment of benefits form in the provider's favor, was billed for, and paid the doctor for the difference, are no longer in existence for all intents and purposes.

Managed care organizations include health maintenance organizations (HMOs), preferred provider organizations (PPOs), and other hybrid forms, including point of service plans (POSs). The purpose of managed care organizations, according to their enabling statutes, is to transfer the financial risks of health care from the patients to the managed care organization. (See Title 42 of the United States Code Section 300e (42 USC Sec. 300e).)

The principal defining factor of managed care organizations is that the managed care organization receives a fixed fee (usually monthly) from each patient enrolled under the terms of a contract to provide specified health care if needed. The managed care organization keeps the fee even if a plan member never or rarely gets sick. Even if a member becomes expensively ill, the managed care organization is responsible if the costs exceed the fees paid.

There are several models of managed care organizations. There are staff model HMOs, in which the HMO owns and operates its own hospitals and facilities, and employs the doctors, nurses, and other necessary personnel directly. There is the independent practice association model of HMO, in which the HMO contracts with individual physicians in private practice (and with hospitals), through which the HMO's members receive medical services. There is the group model of HMO, similar to the preceding model, except the HMO contracts with one or more—usually several—physician practice groups to provide services to members.

A PPO is largely similar to a group model HMO. Many health-care plans offer each participant two or more tiers of coverage, with varying benefit levels, copayments, and flexibility relative to appointments with specialists and receiving care from out of network providers.

Often the physician lists will be the same for all options. Sometimes, due to demand and costs of contracts between a medical group and a managed care organization, a medical group or individual physicians that were formerly available through the HMO option may, on a renewal of a plan (which usually occurs annually for employer sponsored plans), only be available under the PPO or POS option. Maintaining an ongoing physician-patient relationship with a doctor may be important to you. Sometimes, but not always, when such changes occur, the plan and the physician will agree that preexisting patients under the HMO option can continue to use the physician as the primary care physician under the HMO level of coverages and copayments. If your plan does not, you may wish to consider exercising the PPO or POS option in order to be able to maintain your physician-patient relationship.

Another issue involving your choice of HMO, PPO, or POS depends on whether your plan requires females to go through a general practitioner or family practice or other primary care physician in order to obtain gynecological services. Many plans are beginning to recognize that female patients (legitimately) object to such a requirement. They now permit females to visit their gynecologist for routine examinations on permitted intervals without getting a referral from the general practitioner or family practice physician who otherwise is the *gatekeeper* to services by specialists.

Antidiscrimination Statutes

The 1996 *Health Insurance Portability and Accountability Act* prohibits both issuers of health insurance policies and administrators of managed care plans from discriminating against any person on the basis of health factors. (See 42 USC Sec. 300gg-1(a) and Title 29 of the Code of Federal Regulations Section 2590.702 (29 C.F.R. Sec. 2590.702).) No person can be denied eligibility for health insurance or participation in a managed care plan or charged a higher premium based on his or her medical condition (including physical and medical illness), claim experience, receipt of health care, medical history, genetic information, or evidence of insurabililty or disability.

Employers are not required by law to offer health-care coverage to their employees, but if they do, discrimination is prohibited by law—for example, exclusion from coverage of birth control devices from a prescription drug plan because the exclusion discriminates against female employees.

Medigap Coverage

Medigap coverage is supplemental coverage that persons may purchase to provide benefits when available Medicare benefits have been exhausted. (See 42 USC Sec. 1395ss(p).) Medigap policies include supplemental hospitalization coverage that applies when allowable Medicare hospitalization coverage ends.

Policies must conform to one of the several model policies approved by the National Association of Insurance Commissioners (NAIC). The model forms require insurers to provide, at minimum, a core benefit package to the same extent as would be covered by Medicare but for exhaustion of Medicare benefits.

Medical Necessity

Health insurance policies (and services provided by managed care plans) typically cover costs of services that are *medically necessary.* This generally means those services that have been established as safe and effective and furnished in accordance with generally accepted professional standards to treat an illness, injury, or medical condition. Inpatient care for medical observation, evaluation, or other care that could be provided on an outpatient basis will not be considered medically necessary.

Other phrases commonly used in the insuring agreements of health insurance policies to express the same concepts are *reasonable and necessary expenses* and *usual and customary expenses.* Regardless of the phraseology used, because these terms appear in insuring agreements, they are subject to the general rule that an interpretation that results in coverage is to be favored over one that does not.

In conjunction with the medical necessity provisions, there are usually some form of preapproval or prior authorization requirements that apply to certain categories of treatments or procedures. Physicians and hospitals are usually, but not always, familiar with such requirements and they often, but not always, take care of the preapproval processes. If you have any doubt whether your physician has or will take care of these procedures for you, confirm with him or her. This arguably is one of the advantages of managed care plans. The *gatekeeper* physicians must know these procedures and get approval before they even discuss further treatment with you in most cases.

Preexisting Condition Provisions

Many health policies contain limitations on preexisting conditions. Preexisting conditions coverage limitations in group policies and managed care plans are regulated by federal law. (See 42 USC Sec. 300gg(a).) Under these laws, a preexisting condition exclusion is valid only if it relates to conditions for which the insured received care or care was recommended within six months before the enrollment dates. A preexisting conditions exclusion is valid for no more than twelve months, reduced by whatever period the enrollee was covered for that condition under a previous policy or managed care plan. The effect of this latter provision is often to completely negate the preexisting condition exclusion.

For example, an insured covered under an employer-sponsored health plan (Plan A) who changes jobs and becomes covered under the new employer's health plan (Plan B), with no gap in coverage between Plan A and Plan B, is not considered to have any preexisting conditions that would be excluded from Plan B's coverage.

Workers Compensation Exclusion

Most health insurance policies and managed care plans exclude coverage for any illness or injury covered by workers compensation or occupational disability laws. Such exclusions are uniformly enforced, even if the insured did not seek or receive workers compensation benefits. The intent is to avoid multiple recoveries.

Experimental or Investigative Treatment Exclusion

Many health insurance policies and managed care plans exclude coverage for treatments that are not recognized as accepted medical practice or that have not received governmental (*e.g.,* FDA) approval. Often, policies and managed care plans put the determination whether a given treatment is considered experimental or investigative in the sole discretion of the plan's medical director. This is an exclusion that in many ways is a variant of the medical necessity requirement discussed previously.

Coordination of Benefits

Health insurance policies and managed care plans virtually always contain provisions addressing the insurer's payment obligations when an insured has coverage under more than one plan. Think of these *coordination of benefits* provisions as comparable to other insurance clauses in homeowners or auto policies.

Arbitration

Health insurance policies sometimes contain mandatory arbitration provisions applicable to disputes over the recoverability of benefits. Federal law, the *Federal Arbitration Act* (9 USC Sec. 1 *et seq.*) and many states' laws establish a public policy in favor of arbitration of disputes and generally serve as a basis for enforcement of contractual arbitration provisions. Arbitration provisions have been held generally not to constitute an impermissible infringement of an insured's right to a jury trial. Arbitration awards can only be reversible on judicial review if the arbitrator exceeds his or her authority under the arbitration clause—in other words, if he or she decides an issue not within those expressly stated in the clause to be subject to its provisions.

Notwithstanding the foregoing, arbitration clauses must be prominently disclosed in the policy or plan documents and must be stated in clear and understandable language.

Right to Recover Clauses

Most health insurance policies and managed care plans contain provisions governing the health insurer's right to recovery if an insured for whom covered medical care is provided suffers illness or injuries caused by a third party, and sues the third party for damages and obtains a judgment or settlement. Such provisions appear in the policy or plan documents under one or more of the following headings:

- *Reimbursement;*
- *Subrogation;*
- *Liens;* and,
- *Third Party Clauses.*

There are some limitations on the insurer's or plan's right to recovery. The general rule is that an insurer is not entitled to recovery from a third party on a subrogation theory until the insured has been made whole. Arguably, this means that the health insurer in this context would not be entitled to recovery until the insured has been made whole for his or her payment of deductibles and copayments and for any other medical or similar expenses incurred as the result of the third party but not covered by the policy or plan.

This is an equitable principle that can be waived or modified by contract. When, however, such a contractual waiver or modification of this general rule exists, the insurer must pay the insured for a *pro rata* share of the attorneys' fees incurred by the insured's lawyers in the insured's damages suit against the third party. If the insured's lawyers are representing the insured on a contingent fee basis, the insurer is bound by that agreement. Thus, if the insurer had paid 80% of the insured's medical care costs and the insured had paid 20% through deductibles and copayments, the insurer would be responsible for payment of 80% of the attorneys' contingent fee allocable to the medical expense portion of the damages recovery. (The insurer would have no interest in, and no right to recover for damages awarded to the insured for pain and suffering or lost wages, and would have no liability for that proportion of the attorneys' fees attributable to such damages.)

In addition, a health insurer or medical care plan is not entitled to subrogation for benefits paid with respect to any portion of a damages award an insured recovers against a physician in a medical malpractice action.

COBRA RIGHTS

The *Consolidated Omnibus Budget Reconciliation Act* of 1985 (COBRA) (26 USC Sec. 4980B, 29 USC Secs. 1161-1167, and 42 USC Secs. 300bb-1–300bb-8), established certain duties on the part of employers with respect to continuation of health care coverage under employer-sponsored plans when certain defined *triggering* or *qualifying* events occurred. These events are:

- termination of an employee's employment;
- reduction in an employee's hours (that take that employee below the minimum number of hours to be eligible for the employer's health plan(s);
- divorce or legal separation (that is, a covered dependent spouse ceases to be eligible for dependent coverage under the plan because he or she has divorced (or been divorced by) the subscriber or become legally separated from the employee/subscriber;
- the employee becomes eligible to receive Medicare benefits;
- a dependent child ceases being a dependent or exceeds the maximum age for which dependent children can be eligible for coverage under the plan; or,
- the employer files a chapter 11 petition in bankruptcy.

In the event of a qualifying event, the employer is required to notify the employee of his or her COBRA rights within thirty days. The employee has sixty days from the date of the qualifying event to exercise his or her COBRA rights to continue any or all of the employer sponsored health-care coverages. This includes not only the medical/health coverage, but also dental plans and vision care plans.

To exercise the right to continue any such coverages, the insured must tender payment of the full amount of the first month's premiums for all coverages to be continued for the insured and for all dependents, and must do so within the sixty day period. Your COBRA notification letter must state specific amounts in clear language as to how much you must pay to effectively exercise continuation of benefits. If you maintain coverage pursuant to COBRA until you are eligible for coverage under a new employer's plan with no preexisting conditions exclusions concerns.

The premium charged for continued coverage when the insured exercises COBRA rights can include an administrative fee of up to 2% of the full amount of the premiums for the coverages elected to be continued, including all dependents. The premiums on which this administrative charge are based are those in effect for the insured and his or her dependents at the time of the qualifying event.

The insured must *deliver*, not *mail* subsequent months' premium payments to the employer *before* the month to which the premiums apply. The law is unclear whether that means deliver a check or deliver funds (*i.e.,* the check must clear). If you exercise COBRA right, that is your health care until you have alternate health care.

The coverages offered when an employee exercises COBRA rights must be identical to those the employee had before the qualifying event occurred. This means that if the insured elects to continue the health-care plan coverage, all the terms and conditions of the COBRA health-care coverage must be identical to those the employee had before the qualifying event. If the insured/employee elects to continue dental coverage or other coverage previously carried by the employee before the qualifying event, the continuation coverages must be identical to those in existence before.

The available duration of COBRA coverage varies depending on the nature of the qualifying event. Where the qualifying event is a termination of employment, the maximum period of coverage is eighteen months, which may be extended to twenty-nine months if the insured is disabled.

For categories of qualifying events other than termination, the maximum duration of COBRA continuation coverage is thirty-six months. If the qualifying event is the bankruptcy of the employer, the duration of the right to continue coverage under COBRA is lifetime for retirees and widows/widowers of retirees *if* their spouses die before the bankruptcy filing of the employer.

Where the employer's bankruptcy filing predates the death of the retiree, the surviving spouse is entitled to continuation of coverage under COBRA for thirty-six months.

In all cases, when an individual reaches the end of the applicable maximum period of continuation of health-care coverage under COBRA, the health-care plan is obligated to offer the individual the opportunity to purchase *conversion* coverage. Such an offer of conversion coverage must be made within 180 days before the expiration of continuation coverage. The conversion plan offered must be one *generally available* from the provider.

Many states have their own additional statutes and regulations regarding *portability* of health-care coverages. Please see **www.healthinsuranceinfo.net** for specific state questions.

Glossary

A

actual cash value. The price a willing buyer would pay to a willing seller for an item of property. The term applies to the loss valuation portions of property policies.

actuary. An employee of an insurer who performs mathematical and statistical analyses for the purposes of setting rates and for reserves other than loss reserves, such as reserves for incurred but not reported losses.

additional living expense. A homeowners policy property coverage. In the event of a covered loss to the dwelling, the insured generally is covered for the costs of temporary alternate quarters/lodging, among other things, while repairs or reconstruction is ongoing.

admitted insurer. An insurer admitted to transact business within a particular state. If an insurer is not admitted in a particular state, yet does business within that state, it does so as a nonadmitted, or excess and surplus lines insurer. Policies issued by nonadmitted insurers in a particular state are not protected by that state's insurance guaranty fund in the event of insurer insolvency.

agent. A deceptively simple concept. An agent is a person authorized by and on behalf of an insurer to transact insurance on its behalf. Agents must be licensed by each state in which they intend to do business. An appointed agent is an agent for whom an insurer has filed a notice of appointment with the insurance department of a particular state. Generally, an appointed agent is presumed to be acting on behalf of the insurer. That means the person you think of as your agent in most cases is legally the agent of the insurer.

alternative market mechanisms. Programs established by the laws of states to provide availability of insurance to certain categories of hard to place insureds. Examples include assigned risk auto insurance programs.

appraisal. A term with a specific meaning in insurance. Appraisal provisions appear in the loss settlement portions of property policies and are a contractual arbitration provision intended to resolve disputes over the amount of a loss. Coverage questions cannot be decided in appraisal proceedings.

assignment. A provision common to most insurance policies that provide that the insured cannot assign his or her rights and obligations under a policy to another person. This provision enforces the insurer's right to choose with whom it wishes to contract and insure.

B

bodily injury. A liability coverage concept. One of the categories of injury or damage to which liability coverages apply. Bodily injury in the insurance context means largely what most persons think of as personal injury. The laws of the states differ as to whether emotional distress in the absence of physical symptoms does or does not constitute bodily injury for insurance purposes. A spouse's loss of consortium claim is usually considered to be part of the injured spouse's bodily injury damages.

broker. A broker is a person who transacts insurance for another person for compensation, usually in the form of a commission, consisting of a percent of the premium of insurance policies placed. The terms agent and broker are commonly used indiscriminately and incorrectly by many persons, including lawyers and judges. The average policyholder deals with agents of insurers, and usually does not deal with brokers.

building code upgrade coverage. A property coverage that applies to increased costs of construction after loss occasioned by changes in building code requirements since a home or other building was built. Coverage is usually not included unless the insured requests such coverage and pays an additional premium for same.

business pursuits exclusions. An exclusion and definition contained in and relevant to liability coverages under homeowners policies. Business is broadly defined as any trade, profession, or occupation carried on for a profit motive. Business pursuits and activities are typically excluded from coverage under homeowners policies.

C

cancellation. The termination of an insurance policy during the middle of a policy period, by either the insured or the insurer. Many states' statutes restrict insurers' rights to cancel policies midterm. Nonpayment of premium is usually a permitted ground for cancellation, as well as material increase in hazard. If an insurer cancels midterm, the insured is entitled to a prorated refund of premium. If an insured cancels a policy midterm, the insurer usually imposes a ten percent penalty on the amount of the premium refund.

cedent. One of the parties to a reinsurance transaction. The cedent is the insurer which *cedes* a portion of the risk or liability assumed under a policy issued to an insured to a reinsurer and pays the reinsurer a proportionate share of the policy's premium to the reinsurer.

collision. One of the physical damage coverages of auto policies. Collision generally is defined as the upset of or contact of an insured vehicle with another vehicle or object.

comprehensive. The other physical damage coverage of auto policies. Some insurer's comprehensive coverage is limited to certain named or listed perils. It is more common for comprehensive coverage to be stated in terms of accidental direct physical loss, unless excluded.

concurrent causation. Also referred to as multiple causation. A concept applicable to property coverages. Coverage issues can arise when a noncovered and a covered cause of loss combine to result in loss or damage. Most states use an efficient proximate cause analysis to determine whether coverage exists in such a situation. The efficient proximate cause of loss is referred to as the predominant cause. If the efficient proximate cause of loss is covered, the loss is covered, and the obverse.

cooperation clause. Cooperation clauses appear in both property and liability policies. An insured's breach of a cooperation clause can result in a denial of coverage if the insurer can show that it was actually and substantially prejudiced by the insured's lack of cooperation. In the liability context, the purpose of the cooperation clause has been stated to assist the insurer's defense of a suit against the insured, and to prevent collusion between the insured and the claimant.

D

declarations. That portion of a policy that identifies the policy to the insured. The declarations, or declarations page, show who the insurer is, the policy number and policy period, who the named insured is, its mailing address, the address of premises insured, the coverages afforded, the policy limits applicable to each coverage, the deductible(s), and often, the forms contained in the policy.

duty to defend. One of the two principal promises of the insurer under liability coverages. The insurer is obligated to defend suits against the insured seeking damages potentially covered by the policy. Under most policies the average person will purchase, the costs of defense are in addition to, and not included within the liability limits. In most cases, the insurer selects defense counsel.

duty to indemnify. The second principal promise of the insurer under liability coverages. The insurer is generally obligated to pay settlements or judgments when the facts proved show that the damages sought are actually within the policy's coverage.

E

efficient proximate cause. *See concurrent causation.*

examination under oath. A loss settlement condition, usually in property policies. The policy give the insurer the right to demand an examination under oath of the insured, outside of the presence of any other insured. The insured must sign a transcript of the examination. The insurer may request that the insured produce documents and records at the examination under oath, even if the insured has previously provided the insurer with the same records. An insured's refusal to submit to an examination under oath after the insurer requests same furnishes the insurer with grounds to deny the claim.

exception. An exception to an exclusion restores coverage taken away by the exclusion. An exception to an exclusion cannot create coverage for a loss not covered by the insuring agreement of the policy.

exclusion. A policy provision that takes away a portion of coverage extended by a policy's insuring agreement. Under the law of most states, insurer drafted exclusions are narrowly construed and the insurer bears the burden of proving the application of an exclusion.

excess insurance. Excess policies apply upon the exhaustion of the limits of liability of underlying primary insurance. Exhaustion means that the full limits of the primary insurance have been paid for covered settlements or judgments against the insured. Umbrella policies are excess policies that provide gapfilling coverage. Coverage will apply to damages covered under the umbrella policy's insuring agreement that are not covered under underlying primary insurance, subject to the insured's retention (similar to a deductible).

excess lines insurer. See *admitted insurer.*

excess lines broker. An intermediary to whom a retail agent or broker turns to obtain a policy from a nonadmitted or excess or surplus lines insurer. Under most states laws, an excess or surplus lines policy can be issued only upon proof that standard lines admitted insurers will not write a policy for the risk in question.

F

Federal Flood Insurance Program. A federal program that affords flood insurance policies to persons living in areas potentially subject to flood losses. Flood is a standard exclusion from property policies. Therefore, unless one has a policy from the Federal Flood Insurance Program, one will not have coverage for a flood loss. There is a 30-day waiting period after the date of application before a policy under the Federal Flood Insurance Program goes into effect.

first party insurance. Insurance in which the insurer's obligation is to make payment to the insured, as opposed to someone who is not a party to the contract (policy). Common examples are the dwelling and personal property coverages, and collision and comprehensive coverages of an auto policy.

G

general agent. A general agent is a much different concept than that of a retail agent. In the property/casualty context, some insurers contract with general agents to perform underwriting and claims functions rather than to hire their own employees to perform the underwriting and claims functions. In other circumstances, insurers contract with general agents to perform underwriting functions only, commonly for limited classes of business, such as restaurant policy programs. In the life insurance context, insurers sometimes contract with general agents to be their exclusive marketing channel for the insurer's products. In order to sell that company's products, an agent must be a subagent of the general agent.

I

insuring agreement. The insuring agreement, or coverage grant, of a policy or coverage, states the basic scope of coverage. Exclusions then limit or subtract from the general statement of coverage of the insuring agreement. Insuring agreements are generally broadly construed, and the insured bears the burden of proof that his or her claim comes within the basic scope of coverage of the insuring agreement. If a claim does not come within the insuring agreement, there is no need to consider exclusions.

L

limitation on suit clause. A property policy condition that requires a suit on a policy to be brought within a certain time, usually one or two years from the date of loss. These clauses are in effect contractual statutes of limitation, and are enforced. Under many states' laws, the time between the insured's notice of the claim to the insurer and the time of the insurer's claim decision does not count toward the expiration of the suit limitation period.

loss payee. A person, such as a mortgagee or seller of an item of personal property under an installment contract, who is added to coverage as to the building or item of property as an additional insured to the extent of their interest in the property and/or unpaid loan balance.

M

managing general agent. See *general agent.*

multiple causation. See *concurrent causation.*

N

no-fault insurance. A form of auto insurance mandatory in twelve states, and optional in several others. Under no-fault coverage generally, the insured looks to his or her own insurer for bodily injury claims that fall below a certain threshold and cannot sue a third party for damages. Persons living in no-fault jurisdictions should consult with their department of insurance for state specific no-fault information.

nonadmitted insurer. See *admitted insurer.*

nonowned auto. An auto, not owned by an insured and not specifically described and rated in the insured's auto policy, such as a rented or borrowed auto, used by an insured person with the permission of its owner. Nonowned autos are usually defined as vehicles not regularly available to or furnished to an insured person.

nonrenewal. A refusal by an insurer to continue coverage under a policy at its expiration. Most states restrict an insurer's right to nonrenew personal lines policies.

O

occurrence. A liability coverage concept applicable to bodily injury and property damage coverage. Under most American liability policies, occurrence is defined as a accident. The occurrence or accident refers to the liability producing act, not the resulting injury or damage. Under the law of most states, if the liability producing act was intentional, resulting injury or damage is not covered, even if the particular injury or damage was not expected by the insured.

P

personal injury. A group of liability coverages including such things as libel and slander, false imprisonment, and violation of a person's right of privacy. Personal injury does not include bodily injury, sickness, or disease.

personal injury protection. The formal name for no-fault auto coverage.

premium. The amount of money charged by an insurer to issue a policy. Premiums are determined by the insurer's application of a rate against an exposure factor. For example, an insurer might charge a different rate for auto liability coverage for a person who has a greater number of miles driven annually than one who drives less. An insurer might charge a higher rate for premises liability coverage for an auto repair shop than for a stationary store.

primary insurance. Insurance that applies to a loss on a first dollar basis. For example, the liability coverage of a homeowners policy is primary insurance. If the insured has a personal umbrella policy, its coverage would apply as excess insurance upon exhaustion of the limits of liability of the homeowners policy.

professional services. A definition and exclusion common to the liability coverages of homeowners and businessowners policies. Professional services are not limited to traditional learned professions such as law, medicine, and accounting and include any activity that requires specialized skill and training.

proof of loss. A document that must be submitted by an insured in support of a loss under the property coverages of a policy. It must be signed and sworn to by the insured. It usually requires a complete inventory of all property for which claim is made and its value.

property damage. A liability coverage. Standard liability policies cover the insured's obligation to pay damages to others because of property damage caused by an occurrence. Property damage typically refers to physical injury to tangible property.

public adjustor. A person who contracts with an insured to represent the insured in the resolution of property insurance claims. The public adjustor may perform a variety of functions, including assisting the insured in preparation of the proof of loss and such other things as obtaining repair estimates from contractors. Public adjustors are usually compensated by receipt of a percent, often ten percent, of the insurer's loss payment.

R

rate. A basic charge for a loss exposure. An insurer determines the premium to charge for a particular coverage by multiplying the rate against an exposure factor. For example, a common liability exposure factor for premises liability coverage for light occupancy risks such as office exposures is square footage of the insured's premises. Many persons use *rate* or *rates* when what they really mean is premium.

reinsurance. A contract of reinsurance is one by which an insurer procures a third person to insure against loss or liability by reason of such original insurance. The purpose of reinsurance is the spreading of risk, so that in the event of a catastrophic loss, no single insurer's financial condition is likely to be seriously impaired. Without delving too deeply into the issue of insurance industry accounting and regulation, reinsurance enables a given insurer to issue more policies than it could in the absence of reinsurance. Insurance commissioners generally limit the amount of insurance an insurer may write by comparing the ratio of written premium to policyholders' surplus. An insurer is allowed to reduce the amount of its written premium by the amount of reinsurance premiums ceded (i.e., for accounting purposes, an insurer is allowed to credit reinsurance premiums ceded against written premium). This lowers the written premium to policyholders' surplus ratio, enabling the insurer to write more policies.

Reinsurance has an extensive vocabulary specific to that particular part of the business. The original insurer is referred to alternately as: the *reinsured*; the *ceding insurer*; or the *cedent*. The reinsurer is referred to as: the *reinsurer*; or, rarely, the *assuming insurer*.

Reinsurers often retrocede a portion of the liability they assume under their contract of reinsurance with the cedent to a retrocessionaire. This is done for the same risk spreading reasons as between insurers and reinsurers.

A contract of reinsurance is a separate contract from the original policy issued to the insured. A typical reinsurance contract calls for payment by the reinsurer to the reinsured only upon proof of payment by the insurer of a loss to the original insured. Under a contract of reinsurance, the reinsurer accepts a portion of the liability that the original insurer has assumed under the contract of insurance issued to the insured, in exchange for a proportion of the original premium, less a ceding commission. The amount of the ceding commission typically has either two or three components, depending on whether the contract of reinsurance was procured by the insurer with or without the assistance of a reinsurance intermediary or broker. If the reinsurance contract was placed directly by the insurer with the reinsurer, the ceding commission consists of the original commission that the original insurer pays to the producing broker or agent, plus an override commission. If the contract of reinsurance was procured through use of a reinsurance intermediary, the ceding commission will consist of the original commission, an override commission, plus a brokerage commission.

replacement cost. A property insurance concept. Replacement cost coverage applies only if the insured has maintained policy limits that bear a minimum insurance to value relationship to the actual replacement cost. That percent is often 80% but can be greater. Losses are paid on an actual cash value until actual repair and replacement has been completed. Replacement cost coverage usually does not include coverage for increased costs of construction to comply with changes in building codes unless the insured has separately requested and paid for such coverage.

reserves. Reserves are the various accounts in which insurers hold (and invest) funds. Because premiums are payable in advance, insurers must maintain unearned premium reserves for that portion of premiums it holds for which the period of coverage has not yet occurred. Insurers must maintain loss reserves for known losses. In connection with known losses, insurers also must maintain loss adjustment reserves for the costs of investigating and/or defending claims. Because the business of insurance is unpredictable, insurers also establish and maintain reserves for incurred but not reported losses.

S

subrogation. An insurer's right to recover the amount of a loss payment it has made to or on behalf of its insured to a third party responsible for causing the loss. An insurer's right of subrogation arises as a matter of law, although many policies include subrogation clauses.

surplus lines insurer. *See admitted insurer.*

T

third party insurance. Also known as liability insurance. Insurance where the insurer assumes the liability to pay damages on behalf of an insured to a third party for a covered event, such as bodily injury or property damage.

U

umbrella insurance. See *excess insurance.*

underwriting. The process by which an insurer evaluates an application for coverage to determine whether the risk is acceptable for coverage, and if so, the premium to be charged.

V

voluntary payment clause. An important liability coverage condition. Most policies provide that the insurer has no obligation to reimburse an insured for any payment made by an insured in connection with a claim without the insurer's prior permission.

State Insurance Commissioners

Alabama

Alabama Department of Insurance
201 Monroe Street, Suite 1700
Montgomery, Alabama 36104
334-269-3550
www.aldoi.gov

Website contains online complaint forms, as well as other insurance informa-tion, including insurers' addresses, National Association of Insurance Commissioners numbers, business address and statutory address (if different), tele-phone number, agent for service of process, and the powers held (i.e., lines of business for which each insurer is authorized to do business in Alabama).

Alaska

Alaska Division of Insurance
Robert B. Atwood Building
550 West Seventh Avenue, Suite 1560
Anchorage, Alaska 99501-3067
907-269-7900
www.dced.state.ak.us/insurance

The website contains an Alaska Consumer Insurance Guide, a frequently asked questions section, and other consumer information.

Arkansas

Arkansas Insurance Department
1200 West Third Street
Little Rock, Arkansas 72201
800-282-9134
www.state.ar.us/insurance

The Arkansas Insurance Department website contains consumer information, instructions on how to file complaint, rules and regulations, a section entitled, Get Smart About Insurance, and a link to the National Association of Insurance Commissioners home page.

Arizona

Arizona Department of Insurance
2910 North 44th Street, Second Floor
Phoenix, Arizona 85018-7256
602-912-8444 (Phoenix)
520-628-6370 (Tucson)
800-325-2548 (Statewide)
www.id.state.az.us/index

The website contains a homeowners insurance guide, and homeowners insurance premium comparison among admitted insurers.

California

California Department of Insurance
300 South Spring Street, South Tower
Los Angeles, California 90013
800-927-HELP (-4357)
www.insurance.caa.gov

The California Department of Insurance website contains several consumer insurance guides. It also contains premium comparison information for both auto and homeowners insurance that is searchable based on zip code and other underwriting criteria, so that more meaningful price comparisons can be made among different insurers.

Colorado

Colorado Division of Insurance
1560 East Broadway, Suite 850
Denver, Colorado 80202
303-894-7499
303-894-7490 (Consumer Information)
www.dorg.state.co.us/insurance

The Colorado Division of Insurance website includes consumer information, how to submit a complaint, regulations and bulletins (directed mostly to agents, brokers and insurers), and general industry information, including the annual statements of each insurer doing business in Colorado.

Connecticut

Connecticut Insurance Department
P.O. Box 816
Hartford, Connecticut 06142-0816
860-297-3800
800-203-3447 (Connecticut only)
www.ct.gov/cid/site/default.asp

The Connecticut Insurance Department website contains insurance statistics, a ranking of auto insurers by numbers of complaints, and a guide to buying homeowners insurance.

Delaware

Delaware Insurance Department
841 Silver Lake Boulevard
Dover, Delaware 19904
302-739-4251
www.state.de.us/inscom

The Delaware Insurance Department website contains a list of authorized insurers, regulations, and a list of available guides and publications.

District of Columbia

District of Columbia Department of Insurance and Securities Regulation
810 First Street Northwest, Suite 701
Washington, DC 20002
202-727-8000
www.disr.washingtondc.gov

The District of Columbia Department of Insurance website contains a limited section of consumer tips.

Florida

Florida Department of Financial Services
Office of Insurance Regulation
200 East Gaines Street
Tallahassee, Florida 32399-0333
800-342-2762
www.fldfs.com

This site has very little consumer oriented insurance information.

Georgia

Georgia Insurance and Safety Fire Commissioner
2 Martin Luther King, Jr. Drive
West Tower, Suite 704
Atlanta, Georgia 30334
800-656-2298
www.inscomm.st.ga.us.

The Georgia Insurance Department website enables the user to submit questions online, and has an online complaint form. It also contains auto insurance rate comparisons, and an advice and frequently asked questions section.

Hawaii

Hawaii Division of Insurance
P.O. Box 3614
Honolulu, Hawaii 96811
808-586-2790
www.state.hi.us/dcca/ins

The Hawaii Department of Insurance website contains insurance statistics and a personal auto insurance information brochure.

Idaho

Idaho Department of Insurance
P.O. Box 83720
Boise, Idaho 83720-0043
208-334-4250
www.doi.state.id.us

The Idaho Department of Insurance website contains a consumer assistance section and a list of available publications.

Illinois

Illinois Department of Insurance
James R. Thompson Center
100 West Randolph Street, Suite 5-570
Chicago, Illinois 60601-3251
312-814-2427
320 West Washington Street
-or-
Springfield, Illinois 62767-0001
217-782-4515
www.inw.state.il.us

The Illinois Department of Insurance website includes consumer information about homeowners, auto and health insurance, and instructions on how to file a complaint.

Indiana

Indiana Department of Insurance
311 West Washington Street, Suite 300
Indianapolis, Indiana 46204-2787
317-232-2385
www.in.gov/idoi

The Indiana Department of Insurance website contains a listing of available consumer services and company information.

Iowa

Iowa Insurance Division
330 Maple Street
Des Moines, Iowa 50319-0065
515-281-5705
877-955-1212
www.iid.state.ia.us

The Iowa Department of Insurance website contains consumer information, permits filing of online complaints, has an agent search feature, and a frequently asked questions section.

Kansas

Kansas Insurance Department
420 Southwest Ninth Street
Topeka, Kansas 66612-1678
800-432-2484
www.kinsurance.org

The Kansas Insurance Department website contains a shop for insurance feature, and how to file a complaint.

Kentucky

Kentucky Department of Insurance
215 West Main Street
Frankfort, Kentucky 40601
800-595-6053
www.doi.ppr.ky.gov

The Kentucky Insurance Department website contains an insurance consumer page, complaint ratios about insurers, how to file a complaint and insurance company information.

Louisiana

Louisiana Department of Insurance
1702 North Third Street
Baton Rouge, Louisiana 70802
800-259-5300
800-259-5301 (Louisiana only)
225-342-0895
www.ldi.state.la.us

The Louisiana Insurance Department website contains some general insurance consumer information other than how to file a complaint.

Maine

Maine Bureau of Insurance
124 Northern Avenue
Gardiner, Maine 04345
207-624-8475
www.state.me.us/pfr/ins

The Maine Insurance Department website contains consumer information, how to file complaints, and a section entitled, Get Smart About Insurance.

Maryland

Maryland Insurance Administration Agency
525 St. Paul Place
Baltimore, Maryland 21202-2272
410-468-2000
800-492-6116
www.mdinsurance.state.md.us

The Maryland Insurance Department website contains consumer information, a list of available publications, and how to file complaints.

Massachusetts

Massachusetts Division of Insurance
One South Station
Boston, Massachusetts 02110-2208
617-521-7794
617-521-7777 (Consumer Information Hotline)
www.state.ma.us/doi

The Massachusetts Insurance Department website contains consumer service information, including information on auto, homeowners, life, and health insurance. An exemplar of the Massachusetts Auto Insurance Policy is available for viewing and printing.

Michigan

Michigan Consumer and Industry Services
Office of Financial and Investment Services
Ottawa Building, Third Floor
611 West Ottawa
Lansing, Michigan 48933-1070
877-999-6442
www.michigan.gov/cis

The Michigan Insurance Department website contains information on how to file a complaint, complaint ratios, and insurer service of process information.

Minnesota

Minnesota Department of Commerce
85 Seventh Place East, Suite 500
St. Paul, Minnesota 55101
651-297-7161
www.commerce.state.mn.us

The Minnesota Department of Insurance website contains information on how to file a complaint, general information, how to buy homeowners insurance auto insurance claims, and offers a brochure outlining auto coverages and buying, as well as claims.

Mississippi

Mississippi Department of Insurance
1001 Woolfolk State Office Building
501 North West Street
Jackson, Mississippi 39201
601-359-3569
800-562-2957
www.doi.state.ms.us

The Mississippi Insurance Department website contains a limited amount of consumer information.

Missouri

Missouri Department of Insurance
301 West High Street, Room 530
Jefferson City, Missouri 65101
573-751-2640 (Jefferson City)
816-889-2381 (Kansas City)
314-340-6870 (St. Louis)
800-726-7390 (Consumer Hotline)
http://insurance.mo.gov

The Missouri Insurance Department website contains a telephone number list, consumer information, a guide to rates and availability of auto and homeowners insurance, a frequently asked questions section, and a complaint form.

Montana

Montana State Auditor
840 Helena Avenue
Helena, Montana 59601
800-332-6148
http://sao.state.mt.us

The Montana Insurance Department website contains a policyholder service section and a complaint form.

Nebraska

Nebraska Department of Insurance
Terminal Building
941 "O" Street, Suite 400
Lincoln, Nebraska 68508-3639
www.state.ne.us/home/NDOI

The Nebraska Insurance Department website contains a company and agent search function and a complaint form.

Nevada

Nevada Division of Insurance
2501 East Sahara Avenue, Suite 302
Las Vegas, Nevada 89104
702-486-4009
-or-
788 Fairview Drive, Suite 300
Carson City, Nevada 89701
775-687-4270
http://doi.state.nv.us

The Nevada Insurance Department website contains auto and homeowners insurance buyers guides, and how to file a complaint.

New Hampshire

New Hampshire Insurance Department
56 Old Suncook Road
Concord, New Hampshire 03301-7317
603-271-2261
800-852-3416 Consumer Assistance
www.state.nh.us/insurance

The New Hampshire Insurance Department website contains a list of available consumer services and a complaint form.

New Jersey

New Jersey Department of Banking and Insurance
P.O. Box 325
Trenton, New Jersey 08625
609-292-5316
www.state.nj.us/dobi

The New Jersey Insurance Department website contains a consumer guide to auto insurance, an insurance buyers guide, complaint ratio information, and an auto consumer rights question and answer section.

New Mexico

New Mexico Public Regulation Commission, Insurance Division
P.E.R.A. Building
1120 Paseo De Peralta
P.O. Box 1264
Santa Fe, New Mexico 87501
505-827-4601
800-947-4722
www.nmprc.state.nm.us

The New Mexico Insurance Department website contains little consumer information.

New York

New York State Insurance Department
25 Beaver Street
New York, New York 10004
212-480-6400 Consumer Services
-or-
One Commerce Plaza
Albany, New York 12257
518-474-6600
www.ins.state.ny.us

The New York Insurance Department website contains information about New York no-fault auto insurance.

North Carolina

North Carolina Department of Insurance
P.O. Box 26387
Raleigh, North Carolina 27611
919-733-2032
800-546-5664 (Consumer Services)
www.ncdoi.com

The North Carolina Insurance Department website lists available consumer services and information on how to file a complaint.

North Dakota

North Dakota Department of Insurance
600 East Boulevard, Department 401
Bismark, North Dakota 58505-0320
701-328-2440
www.state.nd.us/ndins

The North Dakota Insurance Department website contains consumer information about homeowners and auto insurance.

Ohio

Ohio Department of Insurance
2100 Stelles Court
Columbus, Ohio 43215-1067
614-644-2658
800-686-1526 (Consumer Hotline)
www.ohioinsurance.gov

The Ohio Insurance Department website contains a list of consumer publications and some consumer tips.

Oklahoma

Oklahoma Insurance Department
P.O. Box 53408
Oklahoma City, Oklahoma 73152-3408
405-521-2828
800-522-0071
-or-
3105 East Shelby Drive, Suite 305
Tulsa, Oklahoma 74105
918-747-7700
800-728-2806
www.oid.state.ok.us

The Oklahoma Insurance Department website contains a frequently asked questions section and the ability to order brochures online.

Oregon

Oregon Insurance Division
350 Winter Street Northeast, Room 440
Salem, Oregon
503-947-7980
www.cbs.state.or.us

The Oregon Insurance Department website contains consumer information in general, and specific sections on auto, homeowners, health, and life insurance, plus information on how to file a complaint.

Pennsylvania

Pennsylvania Department of Insurance
Consumer Services
Room 1701 State Office Building
1400 Spring Garden Street
Philadelphia, Pennsylvania 19130
215-560-2630
-or-
Room 304 State Office Building
300 Liberty Avenue
Pittsburgh, Pennsylvania 15222
412-565-5020
-or-
808 Renaissance Court
Tenth and State Streets
Erie, Pennsylvania 16512
814-871-4466
-or-
1321 Strawberry Street
Harrisburg, Pennsylvania 17120
717-787-2317
877-881-6388
www.ins.state.pa.us/ins/site/default.asp

The Pennsylvania Insurance Department website is extensive and contains a great deal of information—far too much to attempt to summarize.

Rhode Island

Rhode Island Department of Business Regulation
23 Richmond Street
Providence, Rhode Island 02903
401-222-2246
www.dbr.state.ri.us

The Rhode Island Insurance Department website contains mostly business oriented information and little consumer information.

South Carolina

South Carolina Department of Insurance
300 Arbor Lake Drive, Suite 1200
Columbia, South Carolina 29223
803-737-6160
www.doi.state.sc.us

The South Carolina Insurance Department website contains information regarding agents for service of process of insurers, how to file a complaint, a list of guides and publications about auto, homeowners, health, and life insurance.

South Dakota

South Dakota Division of Insurance
445 East Capitol Avenue
Pierre, South Dakota 57501
605-773-3563
www.state.sd.us/drr2/reg/insurance

The South Dakota Insurance Department website contains consumer information, market surveys, a frequently asked questions section, how to file a complaint, and a list of licensed insurers.

Tennessee

Tennessee Department of Commerce and Insurance
Davy Crockett Tower, Suite 500
Nashville, Tennessee 37243-0565
615-741-6007
www.state.tn.us/commerce

The Tennessee Department of Insurance website has consumer guides to auto, home-owners, life, health, tenants, and flood insurance and regarding insurance fraud.

Texas

Texas Department of Insurance
P.O. Box 149104
Austin, Texas 78719-9104
210-463-6169
800-578-4677
800-252-3439 (Consumer Helpline)
www.tdi.state.tx.us

The Texas Insurance Department website contains consumer information on auto, homeowners, health, and life insurance and a frequently asked questions section.

Utah

Utah Department of Insurance
State Office Building Room 3110
Salt Lake City, Utah 84114-6901
801-538-3800
800-439-3805 (Utah only)
801-538-3805 (Consumer Service)
www.insurance.state.ut.us

The Utah Insurance Department website contains limited consumer information on auto and homeowners insurance.

Vermont

Vermont Department of Banking and Insurance
89 Main Street Drawer 20
Montpelier, Vermont 05620-3101
802-828-3301
www.bisca.state.vt.us

The Vermont Insurance Department website contains a limited consumer help section.

Virginia

Virginia Bureau of Insurance
Tyler Building
1300 East Main Street
Richmond, Virginia 23219
804-371-9741
800-552-7945 (Virginia only)
www.state.va.us

The Virginia Department of Insurance website contains a limited frequently asked questions section.

Washington

Washington State Office of the Insurance Commissioner
P.O. Box 40255
Olympia, Washington 98504-0255
360-725-7000
www.insurance.wa.gov

The Washington Insurance Department website contains insurance laws and regulations, a frequently asked questions section, and tips regarding auto and homeowners insurance.

West Virginia

West Virginia Insurance Commission
1124 Smith Street
Charleston, West Virginia 25301
304-558-3354
304-558-3386 (Consumer Hotline)
800-642-9004 (Consumer Hotline West Virginia only)
www.wvinsurance.gov

The West Virginia Insurance Department website contains information on how to file a complaint, West Virginia insurance statutes, and a frequently asked questions section on personal lines auto and homeowners policies and coverages.

Wisconsin

Wisconsin Office of the Commissioner of Insurance
125 South Webster Street
Madison, Wisconsin 53702
608-266-3585
800-236-8517 (Wisconsin only)
http://oci.wi.gov

The Wisconsin Insurance Department website contains consumer frequently asked questions about auto and homeowners coverages and how to file a complaint.

Wyoming

Wyoming Department of Insurance
Herscher Building, Third Floor East
122 West Twenty-fifth Street
Cheyenne, Wyoming 82002
307-777-7401
http://insurance.state.wy.us

The Wyoming Insurance Department website contains a personal auto insurance guide.

Index

D